1. Marriage.

2. Family
   Life.

I. Title.

$4.95

Make More of Your
Marriage

EDITED BY
GARY R. COLLINS

Make More
of Your Marriage

MAKE MORE
OF YOUR MARRIAGE

Gary R. Collins, editor

Word Books, Publisher—Waco, Texas

MAKE MORE OF YOUR MARRIAGE

Unless otherwise noted, all Scriptures are from the Revised Standard Version
of the Bible, copyrighted 1946, 1952, © 1971, 1973 by the Division of Christian Education of the National Council of the Churches of Christ in the U.S.A.,
and are used by permission. Those marked Phillips are from *The New Testament in Modern English* by J. B. Phillips, © J. B. Phillips 1958, published by
The Macmillan Company.

ISBN 0-87680-849-6
Library of Congress catalog card number: 76-2861
Printed in the United States of America

Contents

Introduction   7
Gary R. Collins

1.   Marriage As It Was Meant to Be   11
   Lloyd Ogilvie
2.   Gifts of the Spirit in Marriage   30
   Louis and Colleen Evans
3.   A New Look at Christian Husbands   41
   Larry Christenson
4.   A New Look at Christian Wives   51
   Gladys M. Hunt
5.   Reasons Marriages Fail—Communication   65
   Mark W. Lee
6.   Divorce and Remarriage: A Fresh Biblical Perspective   83
   Dwight H. Small
7.   Divorce and Remarriage: Practical Implications for the Church   96
   Lars I. Granberg

8.   Rapid Treatment for a Troubled Marriage   108
     Andre Bustanoby

9.   A Model for Marital Therapy   122
     Donald F. Tweedie, Jr.

10. Training Christian Couples for Marriage Counseling 134
     Norman G. Wakefield

11. The Church and Marriage Enrichment   144
     H. Norman Wright

12. A Christian Perspective on Alternative Styles of Mar-
     riage   157
     John Scanzoni

     Study Guide   169
     Gary R. Collins

Introduction

Traditional marriage is far from obsolete! In the United States alone roughly 2 million people get married every year, and most of these marriages, for better or worse, survive for life.

But marriage *is* changing and the changes are shaking up a lot of people. Many would agree (although perhaps reluctantly) with Alvin Toffler, who argued in his best-selling *Future Shock* that traditional marriage is proving to be less and less capable of "delivering on its promise of lifetime love." To expect a marriage to last indefinitely under modern conditions, Toffler wrote "is to expect a lot. To ask love to last indefinitely is to expect even more. Transience and novelty are both in league against it." As a result, couples are experimenting with new types of relationships—like trial marriages, cohabitation (living together without getting legally married), mate swapping, communal living, and "marriages" between members of the same sex. Divorce, which only a few years ago was condemned or at best frowned upon, has become commonplace and accepted even within the church. Increasing numbers of those couples who do remain together have begun experimenting with ways to banish the "marriage blahs," and keep their relationships alive and growing. Marriage clinics, marriage enrichment seminars, and books on marriage improvement have all become increasingly popular during the past few years; and so have marriage counseling and last ditch attempts to keep troubled marriages from collapsing.

In a report published several years ago, 75 percent of those surveyed considered their marriages a failure and their homes unhappy. Statistics like this have long concerned community, professional and church leaders, many of whom have struggled with the question of how marriages can be improved. This was a major concern of over two thousand people who gathered recently in St. Louis for a week-long Continental Congress on the Family. Planned and directed by J. Allan Petersen, president of Family Concern, Inc., the congress participants met to hear papers and discuss a number of family-related issues, including the changing state of modern marriage.

The chapters which comprise this book were all prepared originally for presentation at the congress, and subsequently revised for publication. Each of the writers was invited to participate because of his or her expertise in family-related matters, deep Christian faith, and concern for helping others make the most of their marriages.

In a challenging and stimulating chapter, Lloyd Ogilvie begins the book by painting a concise picture of marriage "as it was meant to be." This is followed by a husband-and-wife team, Louis and Colleen Evans, who present the thought-provoking idea that traditional male-female roles may not be so important in molding marriages as the spiritual gifts possessed by each of the partners. In the two chapters which follow, Larry Christenson and Gladys Hunt take a look, respectively, at Christian husbands and Christian wives.

The six chapters which follow consider marriage problems and how these can be corrected or prevented. One of these problems, an inability to communicate, is discussed in very practical ways by Mark Lee. Dwight Small and Lars Granberg follow this with discussions of the biblical teachings on divorce and some practical perspectives on how to help those whose marriages have failed. Andre Bustanoby and Donald Tweedie, both of whom are marriage counselors, follow with some practical advice on how troubled marriages can be helped. According to Norman Wakefield, much of this help can come from Christian laymen who are trained in counseling skills and sensitive to the needs of those who have troubled marriages.

Perhaps one of the ways to make marriages better is for churches to develop marriage enrichment programs similar to those described by Norman Wright in his chapter. Regardless of the church's involvement (or lack of involvement) in marriage enrichment, however, traditional ideas of matrimony are changing. Some of these changes are outlined by John Scanzoni in his concluding chapter. It is a sobering analysis and one which should be pondered carefully by every person—Christian or nonbeliever, married or single—who is concerned with the future of marriage as an institution.

To stimulate thought and discussion, a study guide appears in the back of the book. Included with this is a series of questions designed to help church leaders rethink their ministry to married people within the congregation and community.

Marriage may be changing but it is not a dead institution. Many husbands and wives may be unhappy—at least part of the time—but their marriages need not be miserable. The chapters in this book are meant to stimulate churches to help people with their marriages. But more important, this book has been prepared for all those who want to make more of their marriage.

GARY R. COLLINS

I

Marriage As It Was Meant to Be

LLOYD OGILVIE

Recently, I asked twenty-five clergy of a variety of denominations, in representative cities and towns of varying sizes, serving congregations inclusive of a broad spectrum of American culture, to evaluate what they found to be the most crucial problems faced by the people in their congregations. I was not surprised that the majority of responses included marriage and the family.

In conferences and retreats across the nation, I often take an inventory of the participants to evaluate the greatest concerns in their lives. The question I ask repeatedly is, "In what area of your life do you need to experience and express the power of Christ?" Without exception, the responses have been "In my marriage," "In communicating in my marriage," "In my family."

I tried somewhat the same survey in my own congregation in Hollywood. I wanted to build the content of a Lenten series of Wednesday evening meetings around the deepest needs of my people. There is nothing more foolish than answering an unasked question and nothing more powerful than a clearly articulated, personally illustrated, biblically rooted answer to the central ques-

LLOYD J. OGILVIE is the senior pastor of the First Presbyterian Church, Hollywood. Before that he held pastorates in Bethlehem, Pennsylvania, and Winnetka and Gurney, Illinois. Mr. Ogilvie is a recognized leader in experimental forms of church life and innovative methods of training laity for ministry. He is the author of several books, including Let God Love You and Life Without Limits. He and his wife Mary Jane have three children.

tions people are asking. In preparation, on successive Sundays we passed out cards on which each person could write what he discerned to be his most pressing need. The response was overwhelming. Many of the evangelical Christians in my congregation expressed that their most excruciating problems were in their marriages. They found it most difficult to share what they believed in their homes, found their relationship with their mates to be one of the most challenging in which to express Christ's love, and found the greatest contradiction to their commitment to Christ in the kind of persons they were in their marriages. Needless to say, that series and subsequent programs have been established to meet this expressed need.

The church in America has hit wide of the mark in its inability to be personal, practical, and penetrating in healing what I call the hidden malignancy of contemporary Christians. If the church is to be a healing community in which people's emotional needs are met by Christ, and an equipping center for the ministry of the laity to be faithful in society's central structure, the family, then congregations must become laboratories of life in which remedial, reconciling, renewing help is given to enable people to discover Christ's strategy in their marriages.

The virulent virus of religion flows in the bloodstream of the body of Christ in America. As man's effort to win, placate, please, or serve a power greater than himself, religion blocks the jugular vein of Christ's grace. Many congregations have become more religious than gracious. The result is a bland conceptualism, a competitive self-righteousness, and a compulsive pretense to measure up. The gospel has been replaced by a contemporary allegiance to self-generated goodness and propriety. Consequently, the local church is often the last place where people can be themselves, expose their needs, experience the reorientation of their values around the mind of Christ, explore the healing of their emotional wounds, and exchange honestly about difficulties in their relationships. We are not personal enough to illustrate the impact of the gospel to help people see what Christ could do with them and their marriages.

In seminars for Christian divorced persons around the country, I have tabulated the effectiveness of the congregations of which these people were a part. Many of them found their pastors concerned and loving, but often ill-equipped to help them. Church officers were often little help because of tensions in their own marriages. Fellow members were either part of a conspiracy of silence or far too outspoken in favor of the husband or wife. Many agreed that the one comment they had heard from their fellow members was, "I had no idea you were going through this difficulty. You're the last person I would have suspected to get divorced!" Judgment, stigma, a sense of failure, inability to be Christian enough, and sin were communicated verbally, nonverbally, and in the body language of subsequently strained social relationships.

There are many reasons for this. Christian marriage has been ineffectively dealt with in most congregations. We have given too little preparation for marriage, too little help in assisting married people discover Jesus' style and strategy for marriage, and too little remedial opportunity for healing and hope for people who are discouraged and disturbed by the distance between their expectations for marriage and what they are experiencing.

My conversations with clergy in unguarded times of sharing at conferences lead me to believe that marriage is one of the most disturbing problems in their personal lives. Many find their marriages the area of life which most often contradicts what they say and do in their leadership. It is a quirk of leaders that we avoid subjects and implications of the gospel in which we are most ineffective. The nature of the contemporary ministry, with its time, energy, and emotional demands, militates against healthy marriage and fulfilling family life. To whom can a clergyman talk when he faces a breakdown in communication in his home? His superiors in church structures determine his destiny. He thinks that his members demand that he be the "Pastor Perfect." Therefore, he must bank the fires to endure the long, cold night of failure. And what's worse, he must pretend. Church members must do the same with him and with church officers. The hidden malignancy is left to spread its roots into the heart of the body.

We must face this problem honestly in several areas: the biblical meaning of marriage; the discovery of Christian marriage by Christians who are married but have never experienced the lordship of Christ for marriage as it was meant to be; the role of the church as the laboratory for marriage enrichment; and the ministry of the laity in marriage evangelism to touch and heal one of America's aching sores.

THE BIBLICAL MEANING OF MARRIAGE

We must return to Christ himself for the focus of the biblical meaning of marriage. In his response to the Pharisees' questions about divorce, Jesus pressed them back to the roots of God's eternal purpose for life, marriage, and the family. A prayerful and thoughtful study of Mark 10:5-12, when considered in light of the other gospel passages on marriage and divorce, gives a progression to our thought. The recovery of Christian marriage begins with the profound message of the Master. Only what we effectively rediscover can be dynamically reproduced.

The context of the text on marriage focuses our own times. Divorce was easily obtained, resulting in the jeopardy of family life. The Pharisees did not come to Jesus for his wisdom on how to solve the problem of divorce but to pit him against Moses and his commandment. They did not see divorce as failure or inadequacy but as a volatile subject for disputation. The sacredness of marriage was disregarded among the leaders of Israel. Divorce had become so common that it no longer was a matter of concern or conscience. The Pharisees knew that divorce was lawful. Their question was a trap: "Is it lawful for a man to divorce his wife?" Note that they did not ask, "Is divorce the only way to deal with an impossible, broken relationship, when everything else has been tried?" Or, "Is there a possibility of forgiveness, admission of failure, and a chance to try again?"

Jesus' retort sent them back to the very one whom they were trying to expose him as opposing. "What did Moses command you?" The Pharisees' response came as quickly and easily as people repeat the conditions of divorce in our day. They said, "Moses allowed a man to write a certificate of divorce, and put her away." The prejudice of the masculine patriarchalism is obvious immediately—so inconsistent with Jesus' reverence for the nobility of women and the sanctity of the family. Then Jesus had something to say about Moses they had not anticipated. He boldly told them the deeper reason for Moses' injunction: hardness of heart! It was not God's intention that men should change wives like tunics; allowing divorce was Moses' way of dealing with their sin and failure. Jesus' phrase "hardness of heart" described resistance to God, negativism to his love, hostility to his intervention, refusal of reconciliation. For Jesus, a hard heart was a cold, calloused, cantankerous heart. It was no longer open, warm, flexible, sensitive, and free. The Pharisees got more than they bargained for! Now Jesus had their attention for a much more profound message on marriage than they had anticipated.

The key for us is that Jesus' remedy for divorce is not more rules and regulations but the discovery of God's eternal purpose for marriage. What started as a negative disputation occasioned a very positive proclamation. Jesus did not heal the wound lightly; he did not deal with symptoms. He cut to the core of the problem. The same must be true for us. We are not to wring our hands at the divorce statistics but uncover the essential nature of marriage as God intended it. If the church would do that, we could do something about the divorce rate!

When we consider Jesus' message on marriage, we know we are on holy ground. We must not only take off our shoes but open our minds and hearts to allow what he said to reorient our presuppositions, cultural patterns, and prejudices.

Jesus began with the basic purpose of our existence. "But from the beginning God made them male and female." There is an image-shattering, deeper truth here: God made us for himself. Life is not just to get married and have children but to be authentic persons. We are male and female, not only for procreation, but for profession of faith and progress in personhood. We were created persons, not puppets, and given the capacity to know God, love him, and be filled with his Spirit. Jesus came, lived, and died to fulfill our basic need of reconciliation with God. We belong to God! We are to live in fellowship with him as persons in the particular focus of our masculinity and femininity. Reconciliation with him, the experience of his forgiving love, issues forth in the healthy expression of our personalities.

Marriage is not the answer to the dilemma of life or loneliness! If we do not know Jesus, we will never know marriage as he intended it. Our frenzied quest for marriage as the alternative to frustration and unfulfillment is inconsistent with God's plan. Yet in our culture we think a mate is supposed to do for us what only God can do. I believe that is the reason so many people find it difficult to be married and Christian. We have tried to fill the God-shaped void within with a spouse. It won't work. God created us for himself, and our hearts will be restless for him even in marriage. Unless we love God more than our mate, we can never love our mate, really!

This is crucial for our contemporary marriage difficulties. There are no problem marriages; there are problem people who are married to each other. The root of the problem is in our relationship with God. If we do not begin there, there is no beginning of new hope for a marriage. We do what we do because of what we are. Only God's love and forgiveness can heal what we are. Separation from him, rebellion against our purpose to love and trust him, is the cause of our interpersonal difficulties. We cannot love anyone unselfishly or care deeply until Christ has invaded the bastion of our aggressive self-assertiveness. When our hearts have been melted by the love of the cross, when our minds have been gripped by the Good News of the gospel, and when our nature has been filled by the Holy Spirit, then we can be containers and transmitters of creative love in marriage.

The lie of our culture is ingrained in most Christians. We believe that love is a human capacity. Not so! It is a gift of the Holy Spirit. The fruit of the Spirit in love, joy, peace, patience, kindness, goodness, faithfulness, gentleness, and self-control is desperately needed in every marriage. We are not to try to produce these by human effort so that God will approve us. The fruits of the Spirit are given to us because God has accepted and loved us in Christ. We are far too timid in sharing the secret of Christian marriage. It is a Christ-healed, Spirit-filled relationship.

In many years of counseling troubled Christian marriages, I have learned to get to the taproot of the spiritual problem. The personality disorders or distortions can be exposed by the best methods of psychological analysis, but healing begins with an ultimate return to the living, loving Lord for forgiveness and a new creation.

Jesus said, "For this reason a man shall leave his father and mother and be joined to his wife, and the two shall become one. So they are no longer two but one." Oneness is based in the equation of God's purpose for marriage: one plus one plus one equals one! Christian marriage is for three people: a husband, a wife, and our Lord. Christ's prayer for his disciples in the last week of his ministry exposes the yearning of his heart for us today: "That they may be one."

A Christian marriage is not one in which two people who believe in Christ are married to each other. The trouble with many marriages among Christians is exposed exactly at this point. A young woman articulated this distortion to me recently. "I am looking for a good Christian man so I can have a Christian marriage," she said. She is in for painful disappointment if she continues to think that is all that is required for a Christian marriage. The sickness of marriages among so many church people is diagnosed in this fallacy.

Oneness in marriage is the result of experiencing the relational implications of the gospel. It begins with grace. Because of the unmerited love of God, we are made right with him through the cross. This is the focal experience of our salvation. Accepting ourselves as loved enables us to love ourselves as loved by him. This experience of self-acceptance frees a person to be delighted in himself, excited by his own uniqueness and potential. Emotional healing of the syndrome of self-negation and dis-ease is made possible by this experience of grace in the depths of personality. This alone can reverse the "not-okayness" which is communicated through our growing years. Many "Christian" families have failed miserably in being a gracious womb of healthy self-appreciation. Too few children of Christian homes can say, "I'm glad I'm me!" Self-esteem, based in God's grace, is an undeniable ingredient of Christian relationships. We cannot affirm anyone until self-acceptance liberates us for extravagant self-giving. The litmus test of our relationship with the Savior is that we can be to others what he has been to us. Oneness is a direct result. Our Lord is active continually to bring the "wholeness" of our experience of salvation to fruition in oneness in our relationships, but never more so than in marriage. When we know we are loved by him as we are, we can love another as he is; when we know we are forgiven, we can forgive; when we experience the freedom of acceptance, we can be accepting; when we've been liberated from self-negation by a Lord who is for us and not against us, we can be "for" our mates and on their side in the struggle for identity and self-appreciation; when the barriers to our own self-discovery have been removed by the Spirit within us, we can face and confess the barriers which exist between us as people.

Marriage is for oneness: loving expressed in giving. A great Christian marriage is the unrestricted giving of mind, emotion, body, will, and soul to a mate as if given to Christ. A marriage is most Christian, not when it is free of problems and difficulties, but when two persons open themselves to the Spirit of Christ, surrender their wills to him, commit their living to him, and as a conscious dedication, seek to love each other and give themselves to each other as they have been loved and given to by Christ. This is more than making Christ the head of the home. It is the daily, hourly, moment-by-moment willingness to see Christ in our mates and to serve, love, and honor him by what we say, do, give, and forgive.

Only in this way can differences of personality be blended, the uniqueness of each affirmed, the defensiveness of our own rights be healed, and the hurts done to us be forgiven. The miracle of Christian marriage occurs when two minds seek the mind of Christ. Thought patterns, values, preconceptions, and expectations can be unified only as we seek to know and express his mind for us. Another word used to translate Paul's Philippian term, "mind of Christ," is *disposition*. This is thought in personality expression. Our disposition in marriage is radically altered when it is shaped around Christ's person, purpose, and power. An emotionally loving Christian who has experienced the healing of his memories and has actually felt the penetration of Christ's love can express warmth with the gift of his emotions. When the will is liberated to seek deliberately Christ's will with a mate, God can unite two people in profound closeness as fellow adventurers in the new life. Marriage and the family become an expression of the kingdom of God, his rule within, between, and among. In this context, two bodies can be given in unreserved sexual freedom to satisfy, enjoy, and delight each other as gifts of God. That's what Paul Tournier calls "total marriage" and what one of T. S. Eliot's characters tried to express by saying to his mate, "The new person—us!"

A great marriage flows out of this oneness that God intended. He not only created us for himself but for one another as his gifts. Marriage is a supreme expression of this intention. "So they are no longer two, but one." Sin keeps us from this oneness.

But the gifts of God in our mates are often strangely wrapped in the tissues of cultural, psychological, and personality patterns. The honeymoon is soon over, and the challenge of spending a lifetime with another person is formidable. What can be done with our human nature that, regardless of what we believe, is bent toward separateness and bristled individualism? Everyone who is married knows of those things which debilitate oneness.

That presses us on to Jesus' challenge: "What, therefore, God has joined together, let not man put asunder." Often, we have interpreted this statement to mean external forces and persons who wrench apart the oneness God intended for a couple. Or we relegate these words to a defense against divorce. I want to go deeper.

What are the internal seeds of destruction in a couple's relationship which put asunder what God has joined together? Answering this question forces us to consider the dehumanizing and debilitating attitudes, patterns, and traits with which we negate or nullify the oneness God wants to give. Bartered love, hidden agendas, inability to listen, refusal to express initiative affection, determined repatterning of another's personality, manipulative behavior, and judgmentalism are unproductive devices people use to gain control in the "power game" of marriage. The question, Who's in charge here? is beneath the tug of will. The masochism of human nature is nowhere more vividly dramatized than in our distortion of the one relationship which can give greatest pleasure and satisfaction and in our devaluation of the one person who, if loved and affirmed, can give us the greatest ego refortification.

DISCOVERING CHRISTIAN MARRIAGE

Five things have worked for me and my wife in dealing with the hidden things that try to pull us apart. I have also found them extremely helpful to others with whom I speak in marriage seminars and in individual counseling. They are honesty, vulnerability, working contracts, initiative love, and affirmation.

Honesty is not just telling the truth. In marriage it is being open to the truth about ourselves. The persistent work of the Holy Spirit is to illuminate Christ's love and to show us ourselves. The two are inseparable, but the latter is more difficult. This is the daring prayer of the psalmist. "Search me, O God, and know my heart! Try me and know my thoughts! And see if there be any wicked way in me, and lead me in the way everlasting!" (Ps. 139:23–24). He wanted God to introduce him to himself, to excavate deeply and expose the truth about his thoughts. This prayer is a good place to begin to see ourselves in marriage, especially when "wicked ways" is understood in its root meaning of forced labor or compulsive patterns. The psalmist wanted God to get to the bottom of his heart and personality structure to show him the things he did which deliberately opposed God's way for him.

When I pray this prayer and allow God to show me what I am like, then I can see what I have done or been to break the oneness God intended for my marriage. If I begin with myself and not with my wife's faults, tabulated out of an "if it weren't for her" reservoir of judgment, then I know what I must do to change. I can still remember the time I prayed, "God help me!" in the first year of our marriage. I was constantly tripping over the perpendicular pronoun and was not able to love my wife creatively in the language and ways she needed. There was a thick membrane between my emotions and my highly polished rhetoric acquired through years of theological and psychological training. God answered that prayer. I was able to surrender my efforts to remold my wife and began to accept her as the very special and unique gift God had given me. The truly fulfilling and satisfying marriage I have now after almost twenty-five years began the night I asked God to take control of my marriage and make me the man he needed me to be in our life together. I am thankful for the liberating secret he gave me about radical self-honesty because it has enabled me to empathize with people who struggle with problems in their marriages. New hope usually begins for me and them in the prayer, "Lord, change my marriage, beginning with me!"

I have found it helpful to get people to take a clean sheet of paper and prayerfully allow God to guide them in writing down what their expectations of marriage were when they fell in love and were married and what has happened to that dream. Then I ask them to list the things they have done and are consistently doing to debilitate that hope. Only after that do I allow them to write out what they feel their mates have done which disturbs them. Christian honesty is not telling another person his faults; it is being honest before God about ourselves and our failures.

But the next step is equally necessary. *Vulnerability* means that the things we have confessed to God must be expressed to our mates. It's comparatively easy to tell God what we have been, but to expose ourselves to our mates demands even greater courage. It opens remedial conversation, makes way for mutual confession, enables healing, and provides the possibility of a new beginning.

A question begs an answer at this point. People have asked it thousands of times: What if you are willing to be vulnerable and your mate isn't? My answer is to dare to do it regardless. Do it because of Christ's love; do it out of love for the other person; and do it because you love yourself. The cleansing of honesty, vulnerably communicated, will provide the assurance that we have done what love demands to go to the uttermost in seeking a depth relationship.

In most cases, this vulnerability is contagious. It begets a response of openness. If we follow James's admonition to "confess your sins to one another, and pray for one another, that you may be healed" (5:16), the steam of the other person's judgment is let out of the boiler of resentment. It's difficult to accuse a person of the very things he has confessed. The result is introspection and a reciprocity of honesty.

This opens the way to the third aspect of healthy relationships. Honesty and vulnerability can never replace the *true expression of our needs*. A part of loving one's self as loved by Christ is the freedom to be equally open about our expectations. Without this, anger will fester and block creative love.

Marriage is more than a contract; yet a great marriage has contractual dimensions. It is absolutely essential to clarify what two people need and expect from their marriage. Again, writing can be creative. Hidden agendas are destructive, but when husbands and wives can clarify and then talk out what they want, then neither need shadowbox with suppositions. Life's changing demands and the evolving of our personalities necessitate renegotiations of our hopes and dreams. Being Christ's person in marriage does not mean negating our unique personalities or relinquishing the kind of marriage we feel guided by him to desire and work for. If there were more open expression prior to marriage, a more creative give-and-take, some marriages would never be consummated. Because romance often swallows up authentic exchange of goals, people put off sorting out their needs and desires in the hope that life together in the joy of marriage will solve differences. It seldom does. Often it only intensifies them. When this happens, people need help to talk about aspects of their life together which are not satisfying and creative. A new agreement needs to be hammered out and tried together. Most frustrations in marriage come from unexpressed desires and uncommunicated dreams. When these are brought out into the open, a realizable new agreement can be worked out. This needs to be done repeatedly and often. We need to learn the Christian art of negotiation in marriage. There are undeniables without which we cannot live satisfactorily, but there are also secondary desires we should be willing to see as "trade-offs" for crucial needs and wants. A healthy marriage is punctuated by lots of these Christ-centered "bartering sessions."

In the process, people need sensitive assistance in understanding the dynamics of why they chose a certain mate, what are the roots of their image of marriage, and what prompts them to want a particular kind of marriage. For example, I have come to believe that people select a mate in affirmation or negation of the parent of the opposite sex. This is natural, but volatile. With the mixed feelings we all have about parental influence or lack of it, we run the danger of pressing a person into a straight jacket of reincarnated expectation, or we work out unresolved tensions and hostilities of childhood.

I counseled a woman the other day whose father was a tough, hard-hitting baron of industry. He was strong, manipulative, and dictatorial. Her feelings about him were a mixture of anger and admiration. The first prompted her to marry a weak, milquetoast man whom she proceeded to dominate and control. The latter made her dissatisfied with his lack of masculinity. Underneath, her admiration for her father's strength won out, and she proceeded to try to reshape her husband to be stronger and was constantly nagging him for his lack of forcefulness. This woman is a committed Christian, a leader in her church, and a pious person of prayer. What prompted her to seek help were her hidden sexual fantasies of romance with other men and her infatuation with several men with whom she works. All the men who attracted her were strong and dynamic. Because of her deep Christian convictions, she was a burning caldron of guilt and remorse. She had decided that no one who loved Christ should have such feelings and that she was the only Christian who had such fantasies! The truth is that she is legion in most congregations. She needed Christ-guided counseling to see what was happening to her and then become part of a fellowship group which supported her in sorting out the implications of what she discovered about herself and her marriage.

Cultural patterns also contribute to people's image of marriage. We all participate in contributing to the idea that marriage is a panacea and blissful in every way. Most people are left with self-incrimination when trouble begins. They feel something must be wrong with them because they are failing in the one relationship they are given to believe is the answer to all their needs. The pretense of Christian friends incarcerates them in feeling that if they only loved Jesus more everything would be all right. The point is that love for Jesus should provide the freedom to face difficulties and receive help.

Often what little preaching and teaching about marriage that is done in the church sandbags people with the illusion of perfection. We talk a great deal about ideal marriage and little about the dynamics of dealing with our humanity. The love of Christ should free us to see ourselves, honestly consider our wish-dreams for marriage, change what in ourselves is crippling a relationship, and prayerfully negotiate the particulars of life style, values, finances, and family responsibilities.

But all of this is impossible without the gift of *initiative love* and affection. This is the freedom to act on what prayer and creative counseling have revealed. The liberating question which I find breaks the bind of catatonic immobility on dead center is, "If you loved Christ with all your heart, what are the three things you would do to express his love to your mate?" I often suggest a "just because" period of a thirty-day experiment. Consider first what a mate needs and wants. Are these needs and wants creative and constructive? Would they signal to a mate that we are willing to change before our standards are met? The challenge is to do exactly those things "just because" of Christ's love and as an expression of initiative affection. I have seen marriages revolutionized when people have tried this thirty-day experiment.

In a congregation I served some time ago, I gave the "just because" challenge to both the men's council and the women's association. It happened that my talks to both groups occurred on the same day. It was amazing to see what happened in the troubled marriages of that congregation.

Every day can be that kind of day for Christian marriage. The following question is constantly before a Christian who desires to find Christ's strategy for his or her marriage: What can I do to express willingness to change, openness to grow together, freedom to accept the other person, and desire to do the practical or romantic or affectionate things which will delight and communicate esteem?

Affirmation is the sum and substance of all of this. It is the final key to a Christian marriage. We are all starved for affirmation. We dare take no one for granted. Professional success, the accolades of others, and the encouragement of progress in other areas of life will never satisfy the need for affirmation in marriage. Marriage is not to straighten out another person or reshape him to our specifications. It is a God-intended relationship in which the parched places of our lives are watered by the affirmation of love in action. It is Christ in us reaching out to another to communicate that, in spite of inadequacies and failures, he or she is accepted. The desire to be all that our potential affords flows naturally from that affirmation.

The other day a man expressed a very human reaction to this: "Why should I affirm my wife? It will only solidify her determination to be the person I can't stand!" My response was to ask him what he did like about his wife. I tried to help him find the things he could affirm honestly without negating his integrity. It would have been more his problem than hers if he could think of none. He was an elder in the church, and his marital difficulties soured every aspect of his church leadership. But when he tried the liberating power of affirmation, not only did his wife begin to change, but he also began to grow out of the negative syndrome which had blocked the Spirit of Christ in his total life.

The implications of a healthy marriage are profound for the establishment of a creative family. The greatest gift we can give our children is to experience Christ's love in our marriage. The warmth and security will nurture the realization of self-esteem in them. A child internalizes the conflict and frustration of his parents; he will inadvertently reproduce in his own life and subsequently in his own marriage what he has seen and felt. The sickness or health will be "visited to the third and fourth generation."

We cannot deal extensively here with the potent power of the above-mentioned dynamics. They are simply practical, relational Christianity applied to the problems and potential of marriage. We must now ask, How can we help Christians in the church discover Christ's power in their marriages?

THE CHURCH AS A LABORATORY FOR MARRIAGE ENRICHMENT

The missing ingredient in contemporary church people is the lordship of Christ. Many who have discovered Christ as Savior have greatest difficulty in trusting their relationships and the affairs of their living to him. The commitment we made to Christ when we began the new life must be repeated specifically and particularly for marriage. After people have tried to live together and find some semblance of happiness, they are usually confronted with personality problems which seem insurmountable. Our Lord stands at the tightly locked door of our marriages with his loving entreaty, "Behold, I stand at the door and knock; if any one hears my voice and opens the door, I will come in to him and eat with him, and he with me" (Rev. 3:20). In the case of marriage the pronouns are changed from "him" to "them" and "us." Growth in Christ is allowing him to enter, control, and guide all facets of life. There is no greater need among Christian couples than this. The marriage ceremony is so intertwined with custom and sentimentality that even though the reality of the lordship of Christ over the marriage relationship is stated it is not comprehended or appropriated. Only after people have faced the challenge of marriage do they feel the need for the experience of the pledge they made.

The church must discover itself as a laboratory of life for the enrichment of marriage. The life of the congregation must include two aspects. The biblical message of God's intention for Christian marriage must be exposited, communicated, personally illustrated, and forcefully witnessed to by clergy and laity. But equally necessary, the structure of the program of the church must be reshaped. The content of preaching, the curriculum of adult Christian education, the strategy of small groups, and practical conferences on marriage must become the backbone of every program. The health of the church, and subsequently the nation, is at stake!

The pastor is pivotal. He must become open and vulnerable enough to allow the congregation to see that his own marriage is a frontier of his growing faith. This will provide an atmosphere in which Christ's surgery can be performed on the hidden malignancy of marriage difficulties in the congregation. His preaching and teaching should become a spearhead of adventuresome discovery of what can happen in a marriage when Christ is welcomed and trusted completely.

Church boards need to get back to goal-oriented planning for the parish. A page from marketing research will help us ask, What are the needs of our people in their marriages and families, and what can we provide in the parish program to meet these needs? Realizable goals should be set. A basic minimum should include a careful revision of adult education materials and the provision of leisurely, contemplative, honest, open conferences and retreats for couples and families. The church of all places must become a vulnerable fellowship in which failures, needs to grow, and dependence on the power of Christ's plan for marriage can be expressed.

A marriage enrichment conference should include times of teaching, specific witnessing to what Christ has done in the lives of people who have begun the adventure with him in their marriages, and prolonged periods of quiet for individual contemplation and introspection. People need a chance to sort out alone with our Lord what is said. Then they need time together as couples. This should be punctuated by small-group experiences in which people can express both their frustrations and discoveries with other couples who are fellow adventurers and pilgrims on the way to new life in their marriages. Again, writing out expectations, disappointments, and genuine affirmations will help crystallize each person's and each couple's unique situation. Times of dedication or services of remarriage are helpful at the conclusion of such conferences.

These conferences or retreats usually forge a deep bond of mutual concern and supportive love between couples. Often participants need enabling small groups to continue to live out what they are discovering. Like flyers, they need to move from one omi point to another, progressing toward the clarified quality of Christian marriage. A biblically oriented, sharing, caring, praying group makes this possible. People can rediscover where they are, confess patterns which do not work, and get marching orders for the next steps with the Savior in their homes. Study guides, helpful discussion questions, and group methods need to be provided these "churches in miniature."

THE MINISTRY OF THE LAITY

This all has a very exciting evangelistic implication. Surveys indicate that marriage and family problems are infected in the tissues of American life. If the church could begin to help Christians deal with the hidden malignancy, then we could deploy couples for a very needed kind of relational evangelism in the context of marriage. The bridge of relationship could be built to non-Christians to meet their problems in marriage and family life. The aching need in our society is to deploy couples who have found new life in their own marriages. Creative evangelism has always meant sharing Christ in the context of people's particular personal and interpersonal problems.

Some of the most effective lay evangelists I know are couples whose marriages have been healed and who are free to talk with nonchurch couples about what they are discovering. They are broken bread and poured-out wine for couples in trouble and for others who realize in their presence what's lacking in their own marriages.

One couple comes to mind particularly. Their relationship with each other and Christ was on the rocks. They sought help and were led to find Christ's power for their marriage. Now they see that the painful process through which they have passed has prepared them for what Christ wants to do through them with other couples. Everything they go through now, evolving into oneness, is raw material for identifying with others in need. A group of couples meets in their home. Dozens of marriages have been saved through these two. They have been able to lead many husbands and wives to Christ, to a new marriage, and eventually into the church.

The urgency of the church's focusing on marriage and the family is not only to make congregations therapeutic, viable healing centers, but also to prepare couples for ministry in the world Christ died to save. Yet, any thoughtful analysis of congregations in America forces us to admit that we are not what Christ has called us to be to meet this problem. A national renewal movement focused on marriage and the family is badly needed. It is not too late!

There is a need for clergy conferences focused on the church's role in Christian marriage and family life. Pastors desperately need an opportunity to deal with this area in their own lives and in their congregations. We need to begin with ourselves. Nothing can happen through us which is not happening to us. Then the image of the congregation as a healing community needs to be communicated, focused, and modeled. Practical, usable materials for adult education and strategies for marriage enrichment conferences need to be prepared and presented. Clergy must have an opportunity to experience the dynamics of such a conference in order to reproduce them in their own congregations.

If these opportunities for clergy could be regional, pastors could help each other in leading local conferences and assisting in the intensification of congregational programs. Often crossfertilization of leaders is helpful. Pastors could assist in leading conferences in one another's churches. Lay witnesses who are discovering breakthroughs in Christ-liberated marriages could be used to incarnate the viability of what they have been given and serve as small-group enablers. This first step could be followed by a creative approach to family life conferences in which couples could be helped to share with their children what is happening to them. Families need each other to discover the church in the home. Often the dynamics of parent-child relationships can be immensely helped by both adults and children sharing with other families what has both worked and failed in their own families.

What we want to happen in the church in America and in our society must begin with us. The Lord wants to renew our relationship with him and our marriage relationship. We need a new vision of his dream for the families in which we live and for the families we will touch. Boldly we ask for what he is more ready to give than we may be to ask. He desires to change our nation beginning with the strategic unit of the family.

2

Gifts of the Spirit in Marriage

LOUIS AND COLLEEN EVANS

In a day when marriage and family are in radical transition, we, a husband and wife, find ourselves pondering several observations and concerns. We see increasing divorce rate, the rise of "liberation movements," and the antiauthoritarian rebellion tearing down external supports to the family. On the other hand, we are concerned about the internal covenant and commitment relationships which are being lost to the easy-come, easy-go relationships and contracts with ample "small print" that offers partners ready access to the "exits."

We are concerned about how society represses people's creative potential and fails to take the time and expend the energy to discover another's gifts and, to coin a phrase, to "resource" that person to the development of his or her potential.

We are concerned about the roles that are either radical and

Louis H. Evans, Jr., is the pastor of National Presbyterian Church in Washington, D.C. Before that he pastored churches in La Jolla and Bel Air, California. Training and equipping the laity is one of the main concerns of his ministry. In 1975 he was the chairperson of the Task Force on Hunger, National Capital Union Presbytery.

Colleen Townsend Evans is a former actress, and has traveled with her husband in evangelistic work and studied with him in Edinburgh, Scotland. She has written several books including *Love Is an Everyday Thing*. The Evanses have four children.

denunciating reactions to the shortcomings of the past or a return to the rigid, Pharisaical patterns that are often insensitive to individual differences and seem to imply, "I don't care how you feel, just do it the way you are told."

How can we build strong families in light of contemporary situations and in response to the gospel of Jesus Christ and biblical teaching? We are confident that God's own Spirit can and is leading the church to exciting new insights. Such a process will involve much debate and long discussions, but out of it will come guidance and clarity for our day, even as it came for the early church. The following pages express our thinking at this time as we search for a creative answer to marriage and family life.

POTENTIAL DOMINION

Every person has a potential dominion—an ability which can be developed for the common good. From the moment of creation, God made both male and female with potential dominion. "So God created man in his own image, in the image of God he created him; male and female he created them. And God blessed them, and God said to them, 'Be fruitful and multiply, and fill the earth and subdue it'" (Gen. 1:27–28). Every man, woman, and child has some latent ability, some potential dominion over a part, however large or small, of God's creation.

One of the basic responsibilities of the home is to help each person discover and develop these potentials for the common good. This demands intimate and long-term knowledge of the person that comes through committed and covenanted relationships. Without such deep knowledge, persons lack the sensitive, mirroring feedback that allows them to find out who they are. Without a sense of personal identity one feels insecure and will not dare to risk trial and error or the possibility of failure while striving for success. One will usually settle for a "safe route" that denies the exciting possibilities of creative dominion.

Moreover, we humans in our insecurity refuse to let others develop in their strength. The rise of strength in another stimulates a sense of threat and defensiveness in the insecure. These reactions only deter the process of gift development.

GIVING OUT OF ABUNDANCE

We cannot give until first we have received. Jesus Christ set the mold for ministry. He was Creator and Redeemer, but he was also Servant. John states a powerful truth about Christ's base for ministry as he begins the story of the foot washing, the servant role of Christ: "Jesus, knowing that the Father had given all things into his hands, and that he had come from God and was going to God, rose from supper, laid aside his garments, and girded himself with a towel. . . . and began to wash the disciples' feet" (John 13:3-5).

Notice the three statements concerning Christ's own sense of security. *"Knowing* that the Father had given all things into his hands"—he had all the resources he needed for the life of ministry and sacrifice. No one is about to give anything away until that person is convinced there is a source sufficient for life's needs. *"Knowing* that he had come from God"—Jesus had a deep sense of belonging; his roots were clear and firm. His identity and heritage were unquestionable. *"Knowing* that he was going to God"—he had a destination of which he was absolutely confident.

No wonder Jesus could give himself away for the sake of the world. He "had it all together!" He knew who he was and where he was going. He had no identity crisis. That is security! That is the basis of using our gifts in ministry.

The ability to give oneself away on behalf of others is dependent on receiving and deeply sensing that the resources of life are available, on knowing one's heritage and firm background, and on knowing what one's purpose for life is. The persons who are still groping after the basic resources of love and affirmation, who still struggle with identity, who are unclear about purpose and meaning of life, cannot give themselves to others but selfishly clutch at life like a drowning person, insensitive to the peril they foist on themselves and others. They are in a panic for survival.

Parents cannot resource their children, nor spouses their partners, until first they have received. The tragedy is the percentage of insecure parents and partners who attempt vainly to minister to children and spouses out of their own moral and emotional bankruptcy.

Paul Tournier, throughout his book *A Place for You,* speaks of these dynamics clearly and eloquently.

Some parent, realizing with shattering clarity his or her lack of this basic security, may cry out, "What hope is there for me, then?" At times, during the years of heavy professional demands and the normal demands of four emerging teenagers, we too have cried out, "God, we feel so insufficient!" Thank God, the answer always came back, "My strength is sufficient for you," and then God would release the necessary resources. When we took the resources, we were sufficient for the demands.

Jesus Christ gives to any parent or any person that basic sense of *knowing* that all resources necessary for life are in our hands. "I will give you the keys of the kingdom" (Matt. 16:19). "I can do all things in him who strengthens me" (Phil. 4:13). Any parent can *know* that he or she has come from God. "Who were born . . . of God" (John 1:13). "When we cry, 'Abba! Father!' it is the Spirit himself bearing witness with our spirit that we are children of God" (Rom. 8:15, 16). Every parent can *know* his or her call of the Spirit and gift of ministry. In spite of any short-changing or emotional deprivation of the past, we can know God's miraculous power. He is able to fill the voids of the past either through the direct ministry of his Holy Spirit or through the loving lives of his affirming and resourcing people. Thank God for his covenanting people! "With God all things are possible" (Matt. 19:26).

Children who have not received are not only unable to give but restless, striving without consideration for others, aggressive, materialistic, and grasping for physical possessions in an attempt to assuage their emotional and relational needs. They will never be satisfied, of course, until the deeper needs of crucial and accepting relationships are met.

Women who have not received basic affirmation and commitment show their hunger in grasping at "lib" extremes, rejecting normal childbearing roles and home responsibilities; they are strident and hard.

Men who have not received the resourcing necessary for a clear identity and the knowledge that they make happy the important people in their lives are the "what-makes-Sammy-run" kind of executives who spend all their time and energy at the beck and call of the "daddy" corporation, or the laborers who demand beer, slippers, and silence while they watch their favorite TV show.

We must receive before we can give.

A GIFT FOR THE COMMON GOOD

The New Testament teaches that each of us, male or female, receives some gift or gifts of the Spirit when we come to Christ and the Holy Spirit enters our lives. Each gift is given for the common good; it is meant for someone else's benefit, the building up of the body of Christ for its ministry to the world (1 Cor. 12; Rom. 12).

1 Corinthians 12 and 14, Romans 12, and Ephesians 4 are principal passages on this subject. They speak of a gift or gifts given to meet another's need. When all gifts are working properly, the body functions wholly, and the ministry is accomplished in an atmosphere, not of inferiority or superiority, but of cooperation and coordination under the head who is Christ. One task of the church is to discern and encourage the development of these gifts.

The same is true of the home. The Holy Spirit gives to each spouse some gift or gifts of the Spirit for the common good, that is, for the functioning of the home, both for its own sake and for the sake of the world. Therefore, each home should be sensitive to the gifts of each person, aiding the process of identification of these gifts and resourcing the members to develop his or her gift. This is true for spouses and children alike.

This is in contrast to the Pharisaical or rigid process, in which roles are assigned purely on the basis of sex, without deference to gifts. Jesus encountered the Pharisaical insensitivity with his own free life style. He was willing to have theological discussion with a woman (not done!) who was a Samaritan (not allowed!) and who was living in loose circumstances (unthinkable!) (John 4:1–42). He lashed out against the thoughtlessness of the *halakoth,* the "narrow way," of Jewish law that piled heavy burdens on the backs of people as the religious community did little to lighten the load while demanding conformity.

The writings of St. Paul have proven very difficult for many who are working through roles in family life. On one hand he appears to put women down by saying they should not even speak in church; if they have a question, they should ask their husbands at home (1 Cor. 14:33–36). In another place he states that women should be subject to their husbands in everything (Eph. 5:24), effectively denying full use of the gifts in a marriage or even obedience to the Lord should this go against the husband's desires. On the other hand he declares that there is no longer Jew or Greek, male or female, for all are one in Christ (Gal. 3:28) and seems to make no differentiation between the sexes in the gifts of the Spirit. How do we explain such contradiction?

Our belief is that Paul's Pharisaism had continuing influence on his teaching. Now some will vigorously deny that Paul's writings are at all influenced by his former Pharisaism, but why? Other leaders in the church were affected by their pasts in their ministries.

The Apostle Peter was cut off from ministry to the Gentiles for years by his Pharisaical separatism until God liberated him in a vision (Acts 10) only to see him regress into his former behavior out of fear of the Jews who still held to separatism (Gal. 2). James and other leaders were similarly affected by the separatism taught in their pasts. Why not Paul?

The side of Paul we would like to respond to is that which makes no distinction between male and female in the giving and the functioning of gifts. The seeds Paul dropped upon the rock of male supremacy that has held women in subservient position for centuries took root and split the rock, allowing women to find their place as fully productive persons in society. True, there are still roles that are assigned by sex, such as childbearing, and the role of chief breadwinner that usually falls to the male. But these should not deny other gifts that should be free to operate in a marriage.

For instance some would deny the role of spiritual teaching to the woman in marriage, saying this is the role of husband and father. Yet, evidently Priscilla was the lead teacher in her marriage. When first mentioned she follows the name of her husband Aquila. For almost three years Paul lived with them in Corinth as they made tents together and taught the gospel in the synagogue each Sabbath. Then a great teacher, Apollos, mighty in the exposition of the Old Testament, preached about Jesus eloquently but incompletely. Aquila and Priscilla explained the way to him more fully, and from that time on Priscilla is mentioned before Aquila. Evidently Luke mentions persons in order of their spiritual leadership. When first mentioning Saul, he puts him at the end of the list of disciples and apostles (Acts 12:25, 13:1, 2, 7). But after his highly effective disputation with Elymas at Paphos, he is mentioned first with a new name, Paul. In fact his companions are now called "his company" (Acts 13:13).

Paul, in speaking about the church in their home, mentions Priscilla first, even using her nickname Prisca (Rom. 16:3; 1 Cor. 16:19). Evidently her spiritual gift of teaching was not limited by her sex. That is the side of Paul to which we would like to respond. To put a woman in Christ in such a position that her gifts are truncated appears to us a denial of the gifts of the Spirit. She is "helper" to man, yes, but that does not imply inferiority, for the word *azar* used in Genesis 2:18 is that same word used for God as our helper. The curse of subjugation (Gen. 3:16) is removed in Christ, and there is no longer male or female but a oneness and parity in Christ. Some roles are determined by sex, but most are determined by the gifts of the Spirit.

A NEW DAY

Things have changed a lot for women today. "You've come a long way, baby!" First, the modern American woman has been "liberated" by technology from many former time- and energy-consuming chores.

Second, an increasing number of women have been educated for professional careers, thus activating an "expectation level." Moreover, only the "male chauvinist pig" thinks of a woman as a "mindless body" and compliments her primarily for her beauty. Recently while attending a college graduation, we noticed that women walked off with 83 percent of the cum laudes!

Third, we cannot turn back the clock on the feminist movement any more than we can on the racial or ethnic movements, and thank God for that! We must applaud the fortitude of the oppressed who refuse any longer to be oppressed. The person who refuses to let his or her identity be distorted by oppressing patterns is both spiritually and psychologically healthy. He or she follows the example of our Lord who remonstrated strongly when his own beloved disciples tried to make him out to be a messiah after their traditional beliefs and not according to his own identity and God-given call (Matt. 16:24–28). Dr. Martin Luther King, Jr., said that the oppressed are often as guilty as the oppressor because they allow the oppression.

Fourth, world population and the hunger crisis have brought about an abrupt and radical change regarding childbirth in the minds of both men and women of the present generation. No longer do women bear an average of 7 children; they bear 1.9! This changes a woman's time involvement drastically and opens a whole new vista of potential. Put all of these factors together and you have gross change! Deep emotions are involved in this process, and it behooves Christians to do some clear thinking and a minimum of name-calling, which may not be so easy.

We fear two extremes. The one shouts, "Down with mother-hood," denying all the roles indicated by the biological difference. Babies and postpartum responsibilities are put down as degrading and frustrating to the career potential of women.

The other shouts, "Women, submit to your husbands in every-thing." Explicit or implied is the silence of the spiritual woman in regard to sharing her faith in the presence of an spiritually immature husband. We wonder what would have happened to Timothy if both his mother and grandmother had remained silent and waited for his Hellenistic father to come around. There is no indication he ever did (2 Tim. 1:5)! Some even ask Christian women to do the wrong a husband requires, in order to carry out their submission to him. Whatever became of Christ's word that whoever "loves [family] more than me is not worthy of me" (Matt. 10:37)? True, he does not mention husband and wife relationships, but we will include them in the spirit of the passage. We have seen more women win their husbands by standing up for their faith and its responsibilities, and speaking the truth in love, than those who denied the expression of their faith in hopes of bringing him around.

With the first attitude, it will be very difficult for a woman to give herself in service to childbirth and resultant responsibilities of motherhood unless she has first received those resources of life which enable her to accept her identity as childbearer and mother.

In my case, I could not have given myself to motherhood and the great joy of it if God had not filled my cup with his love and acceptance, and had I not known the covenant love of my husband. Without those securities we doubt that a woman can accept a mother identity, and without a clear identity few can give themselves to minister to others.

We would urge women who have the other attitude to think about the gifts of the Spirit in a marriage.

IDENTIFY YOUR GIFTS

One of the first steps in putting gifts of the Spirit to work in a marriage is to *believe* in such a thesis and to enter into the process of becoming aware, sensitive, and on the lookout for indications of your own and others' gifts.

Not all men are gifted in financial management; sometimes the wives are. In many mature and happy Christian homes we have seen the wife take the initiative in financial matters. True, there was always discussion about the decisions, and in the great majority of the circumstances, there was agreement. But in each, there was a quiet acceptance of her gift and an acquiescence to her counsel even though the "man was the head of the house."

Some men are not gifted in teaching; to require them to be the spiritual teacher as "head of the family" would be to put a heavy burden on their backs as well as create an atmosphere of awkwardness in the process, which repels rather than attracts the student. That does not mean a man might not "teach" in his own style of actions and responses to life's situations.

If the wife's gift is discovered to be something that takes her outside the home, then she and her husband need to consider the place of children in their marriage. If they feel children are right for them, then they ought to set aside the time to do the job right without feeling "hemmed in" or becoming the victims of "cabin fever." The mature woman will not feel pushed out of shape or frustrated in the role of childbearing; she will be able to give herself to this process with joy and delight, for this is a phase of her life. If she cannot raise children in this attitude, then for God's sake and the child's sake she shouldn't have children; no one wants to feel unwanted or that he or she is an inconvenience. But so many, not wanting to "make the sacrifice," are yet pressured by the "standard role" and have children, resisting all the way.

And that goes for the husband as well as the wife. Let the father take his responsibility in childrearing. A shocking proportion of men have shown immaturity and a lack of secure identity by spending so much time "in the corporate pursuit" as lackeys to ego-hungry men who demand and have no consideration of the needs of others. These fathers knuckle under, denying their Christian witness as fathers and husbands, and burn themselves out "in sacrifice for their families." How many women or children have said, "I want him, not his money," and they usually come from pretty well-heeled homes. Just a few years ago, one hundred thousand fathers left their "good homes" to get their "freedom," unable to give themselves away. In many instances they were the products of homes lacking the basic covenants and commitments necessary for mature growth.

There are seasons to life, and one season is for childbearing. The greatest product a man and woman can give to the world is a child who "is put together with his head screwed on frontwards, and knows where he or she is going." Belittle that product and you have started the culture down the road to decay.

RESOURCING ANOTHER'S GIFT

But then come the other seasons, those that a new day has made possible. Women take their place in society and business, fulfilling their career potential, perhaps started and then put in moth balls or at least throttled some during the childbearing years. This may mean a new life style for the man. In order to "resource" her for her potential, he may have to pick up some of the domestic responsibilities, demand less of her in entertainment or other roles. To resource another means giving time, energy, money, and whatever else is available and needed.

Since the children have gone on their collegiate way, Colleen has taken up an obvious gift of writing. During the child-rearing years, the gift showed its head on occasions, but limited time and parish demands did not permit its development. But the few things she published showed that "she had the gift." Now Louis has had to cut down his expectations of her entertaining responsibilities.

She is reaching far more by her books. Lou must provide whatever physical surroundings she needs, giving emotional encouragement, and believing in her work and abilities even as she has and still does for him.

Among the children we are noticing now the emergence of gifts. One is sensitive to the medical needs of the family, another to the political and ecological factors of family life, coming home with plans for transportation and energy consumption that have caused us to change our style radically. Another is the mechanic who needs only to be pointed to the task and sails into it with tremendous energy and natural ability. Another is our resident psychologist and counselor, speaking up without hesitation with good insights on family pace and stress, especially that of her father! In each case we as parents have had to let something go for which we formerly held responsibility. In some instances it is great to have the responsibility lifted; in others it is downright difficult to turn loose. But gifts grow by trust and use. That is part of the resourcing process—to trust another and turn him or her loose to "do their thing."

"As it is, God arranged the organs in the body, each one of them, as he chose. . . . joined and knit together by every joint with which it is supplied, when each part is working properly, makes bodily growth and upbuilds itself in love" (1 Cor. 12:18; Eph. 4:16).

The realization of a gift-sensitive and gift-developed home is one of the greatest joys of the Christian life, a model of hope in a day of radical transition and confusion. If more could see this sort of home, they would be attracted to the covenantal and committed life of Jesus Christ and the home which he designed in his loving creation.

3

A New Look
at Christian Husbands*

LARRY CHRISTENSON

Husbands, love your wives, even as Christ also loved the church, and gave himself for it; That he might sanctify and cleanse it with the washing of water by the word, That he might present it to himself a glorious church, not having spot, or wrinkle, or any such thing; but that it should be holy and without blemish. So ought men to love their wives as their own bodies. He that loveth his wife loveth himself. For no man ever yet hated his own flesh; but nourisheth and cherisheth it, even as the Lord the church: For we are members of his body, of his flesh, and of his bones. For this cause shall a man leave his father and mother, and shall be joined unto his wife, and they two shall be one flesh. This is a great mystery: but I speak concerning Christ and the church. Nevertheless let every one of you in particular so love his wife even as himself . . . (Eph. 5:25–33, KJV).

Seated in my study one day, I read this text and suddenly saw something that lifted me right off the chair. "Husbands, love your wives, even as *Christ loves the church* . . ." That's the taproot of God's order for the family! The key to a family's life is the love the

LARRY CHRISTENSON is pastor of Trinity Lutheran Church, San Pedro, California. After studying and working in Germany with the Lutheran Church, he was called to his present pastorate. He is the author of *The Christian Family* as well as a number of other books. Mr. Christenson is married and has four children.

* Adapted from the author's forthcoming book of the same title to be published by Bethany Fellowship.

husband has for his wife because the husband's love is patterned after the love that Jesus has for his church. And Christ's love for his church is its very life!

This led to a very simple question, How does Christ love his church? If I could find the answer to this question, then I would also have an answer to the question, How does a husband love his wife?

Love, as we are using it, is not simply a feeling within ourselves, but rather something that transmits itself into specific action. Thus we must ask, In what specific way does Christ manifest his love and make it concrete and practical? I believe we will find some answers as we consider the various roles in which Christ relates to his church and apply these roles to the husband/wife relationship.

THE HUSBAND AS LOVER

The first role in which Christ manifests his love toward his church is as a *lover* or *bridegroom.* Commitment is the key to this relationship. Jesus doesn't simply love the church because the church is lovable. He loves the church because he has set his *will* to love the church.

Paul Verghese, a bishop of the Syrian Orthodox church, has pointed out that our romantic notion of love, by which a man and a woman are supposedly attracted, fall in love, and live happily ever after, does not come from the Bible, but from the French troubadours of the eleventh century. This view of love is inadequate; it goes on feeling instead of commitment. There is nothing wrong with feelings of "falling in love," but when love sinks its root structure down into the subsoil of the will, it gains a strength and stability. There will be emotions, feelings, and desires, but they won't be subject to the mood of the moment. There are many times when we don't feel like loving, but we can set our will to do so nevertheless.

Once on a TV talk show, the Latin American movie actor Ricardo Montalban was confronted with the challenge: "We know Latins are great lovers, and you have the reputation of a great screen lover. Now, tell us, what makes a great lover?"

The commentator perhaps expected some ribald comment, but

Montalban answered, "A great lover is someone who can satisfy a woman all his life long, and be satisfied by one woman all his life long. A great lover is not someone who goes from woman to woman. Any dog can do that."

That's the love Christ has for his church. It is a mystical reality, and yet it is the basic relationship of total, unqualified commitment.

Ephesians 5:28 shows us in a practical way how the husband is to love his wife. The Scripture says that a man should love his wife as his own body and that he who loves his wife loves himself. How does a man love his own body? One way is that he is *careful for its needs*. He feeds and clothes his body, and he is sensitive to how his body functions. He wouldn't go outside in below-zero weather with only a T-shirt. Likewise, if a husband is to care for the needs of his wife, as he cares for his own body's needs, he must become as sensitive to the feminine mystique as he is to the senses of his own body.

An old Norwegian farmer had been married twenty-five years. One morning after he had done his chores he came in to discover that his wife had not prepared breakfast. When he went to question his wife about the matter, he found her crying.

"What's the matter with you?"

"Oh, I just got to thinking, Hans, you never tell me that you love me. Twenty-five years we've been married, and you never tell me that you love me!"

He responded, "Look woman, I married you twenty-five years ago, and I told you then that I loved you, and if anything changes I'll let you know!"

That may have been enough for him, but it wasn't enough for his wife—she needed to be told that he loved her. A man and woman have different needs.

Second, a man is sensitive to the *hurts* of his body, and a husband needs to be sensitive to his wife's hurts. That means that he doesn't come home from work, flop down in front of the television, and tune out the family. He cannot become sensitive to hurts in his wife's life unless he is willing to listen to her and share in her experiences.

God is aware of the needs of the wife, and he is aware of the needs of the husband. His very purpose in bringing together a man and a woman is that they might complement one another. One of the needs of a wife is to realize how she completes her husband and how he completes her. This applies to many different aspects of their relationship.

One aspect is the sexual relationship of the marriage. This relationship is meant to entail the deepest kind of giving between the man and the woman. A woman needs to give herself to the man and have him give himself to her. This deep giving of oneself reflects the giving of Christ for his bride, the church.

Satan hates sex because he sees that it is something God created as a great gift for man and woman to enjoy within the circle of marriage. That is why he does everything he can to get that gift operating outside the confines of marriage in adultery, free love, perversion, lust, and so on. Whenever a man and a woman come together in marriage, Satan trembles because it is a symbolic reminder to him of the love that Christ has for his church, which spells his downfall.

THE HUSBAND AS SAVIOR

The second role in which Christ relates to his church is that of *savior*. Ephesians 5:25 tells a husband to love his wife "as Christ . . . loved the church and *gave himself for it.*" He is Savior of the church, and that pattern is repeated in the husband/wife relationship. As savior, the husband demonstrates his love in that he sacrifices for his wife.

Some notions of free love abroad in our culture suggest that this love really liberates: to love with no ties, no commitment. Actually that is the most conservative, selfish kind of love one could imagine! It wants to give nothing. It will not risk a single thing. The most daring kind of love commits itself totally to marriage.

There are four words in the Greek language of the first century for *love*. There is the word *storgē* which is the affection within a family and is expressed primarily within the family setting. That word is not used in the New Testament. Then there is the word *eros* from which we get our word *erotic*. That is the kind of love we refer to when we speak of "falling in love." It is a strong, passionate feeling between a man and a woman. This word, likewise, isn't used in the New Testament. The next word is *philia* or the verb *phileō* from which we get such words as *philosophy* and *philanthropy*, meaning the love of friendship and common interests. It is used sparingly in the New Testament. Finally we have the word *agapē*, the love that causes one to sacrifice himself, to give himself up. All four types of love are demonstrated in the relationship between husband and wife, but the love that undergirds and supports the others is *agapē*.

What does it mean to "give oneself up for something"? Jesus said, "If any man would come after me, let him deny himself and take up his cross daily and follow me" (Luke 9:23). This is the principle of discipleship. A husband must sacrifice his rights as an individual to be a disciple to Christ. He says, "I have no rights. I give myself up the way Jesus gave himself up." Jesus had a right as a Jew living in that society to a fair trial, but he gave up that right. He had a right to call legions of angels to his defense, but he gave up his right. He gave up his rights, and out of that surrender, that deep way of the cross, God was able to establish his authority.

After the crucifixion Jesus said, "All authority in heaven and on earth has been given to me" (Matt. 28:18). After the cross Jesus was given authority, and after a husband has entered into the way of the cross, God can entrust him with the authority to rule over his family. Only after he has learned something of the way God deals with ego, the self, is the husband able to help his wife and family in the ways of God.

The Old Testament illustrates this beautifully in the prophecy of Hosea, who married an adulteress. The word of God comes to Hosea, "Go . . . love a woman beloved of her friend, yet an adulteress" (Hos. 3:1, KJV). She had left him to become a prostitute, and now he found her being sold in the market for about the price of a common slave; he bought her back for fifteen shekels and a homer and a half of barley. And he brought her back home. Can you see the neighbors there in Samaria? "Here's that son of a priest, Hosea, coming home in the middle of the day from the slave market with that adulterous wife!"

"Why doesn't he have her stoned as the Law of Moses says?"

"Look at him, he's taking her back. She'll just run off again; that's what she'll do!"

Hosea had to suffer humiliation; he had to give up his pride.

When he did, he was able to speak with authority, "Now you must live as mine for many days and not play the harlot." So far as the records show, Gomer never left him again.

That is the husband in the role of savior, loving his wife, going the way of the cross, allowing God to deal with his own self-life so that he can bring to his family the help, the strength, and the authority it needs.

THE HUSBAND AS SANCTIFIER

The third role in which Christ relates to his church is that of *sanctifier*. When I first compared this aspect of Christ's relationship with the church to the husband/wife relationship, I hesitated because I had always thought that sanctification was the job of the Holy Spirit alone. Then I read the Scripture again: "Husbands, love your wives, even as Christ also loved the church and gave himself for it; *that he might sanctify it . . .*" The parallel runs straight through the verse. It means that the husband helps his wife to become what God wants her to become.

First, he helps her to become *holy.* He has a concern for her spiritual welfare. He is fundamentally concerned that his wife have opportunities to grow and develop in faith so that she becomes all that God wants her to become. He intercedes for her, blesses her, and provides time for her to be alone with God.

Second, a husband is concerned that his wife become *wholly* the Lord's, that is, that she become a fully developed person. I don't want my wife to become like some other wife; I want her to become the woman that God created her to be—intellectually, emotionally, culturally, sexually, domestically, and in every other way. When we realize that God has entrusted our wives to our care that they might become all that he wants them to become, we have discovered our calling as husbands.

THE HUSBAND AS LORD

The word *lord* comes from a feudal setting in which there existed a relationship between the lord and the people who worked his land. The people would come inside the lord's castle walls for protection.

As Lord, Christ guards his church from attack. Likewise, a husband is responsible to guard and protect his wife. One of the basic things he protects her from is economic want. He is responsible to see that she, in committing herself to him, is set free from basic anxieties in this area.

In our culture this raises the question of working wives. Without going into all the "ins and outs" of this question, we can establish a basic principle. In considering this question, the husband and wife should ask themselves, Is the job that the wife might take something which would fundamentally build up the *quality* of the family's life (not simply raise the standard of living)? Is it going to minister to the well-being of the family and to their calling under God? Sometimes we may have to lower our standard of living in order to raise our standard of life. Whether the wife works or not, the fundamental responsibility in providing for the family still rests upon the husband.

Another area in which a husband protects his wife is very obviously the physical realm. He guards her against physical attack. Every culture has written into its folkways protection for its women-folk.

He also protects his wife from emotional attack. A wife is meant to live behind the protective shield of her husband in relationships outward to the community and also within the family. When a child mounts an emotional attack against the mother, the father must deal with it decisively. A mother should never have to battle for the respect of her children.

This came home vividly to me once when I was six or seven years old. I was arguing with my mother about something, and as she went out of the dining room toward the kitchen, I yelled after her, "You're a big dummy." In the meantime, my father had entered the dining room from the other door. I don't think I ever saw him move so fast! He came across to where I was standing, took me by the shirt front, and lifted me right off the floor. "Who's a dummy?" he asked. "I'm a dummy, I'm a dummy, I'm a dummy!" I blubbered. I learned something that day. I learned that I could not abuse my mother without incurring the wrath of my father. He taught me more respect for womanhood in those three minutes than I could have learned through dozens of books and lectures. He protected my mother in that he constantly gave us children the impression of a relationship of total respect, regard, and esteem.

One day I was talking with my wife about the protection that a husband provides, and I asked her what she considered to be some of the ways in which a husband protects his wife. She came up with something I would never have thought of, but which is right on target. She said that a husband protects his wife in that sometimes he says no to her. He recognizes when she is extending herself too far, getting involved in more things than she ought to for her own well-being. He says, "No, you can't do that." That is a protection that a wife needs because by nature she wants to give.

Finally, a husband protects his wife from spiritual attack. Because of a woman's openness to spiritual attack, God has given the whole gift of covering so that she will not have her unique gifts subject to misuse or to deception. In our congregation, for instance, we have had many words of prophecy come through women. Also, some of the really creative thrusts that God has given us have come from the women. These have brought the greatest blessing when the woman has submitted the prophecy to her husband, and the husband has submitted it to the entire congregation. In this way the woman is protected from defending what the Lord has shown her. Her husband provides the spiritual covering.

THE HUSBAND AS HEAD

Let's look finally at the husband's role as *head*. As Christ is head of the church, so the husband is head of his wife and family. As head he directs his wife by giving her intelligent leadership. Whenever the word *headship* is mentioned, our natural reason associates it with such words as *authority, rule, boss, laying-down-the-law,* and so on. However, the first word for the head of the house is not authority, but submission—submission to his head, who is Christ. "The head of every man is Christ" (1 Cor. 11:3). One who is not under authority himself is not able to be a head to his wife. In other words, you can't be a man as far as God is concerned unless you are under the headship of Christ. Only as a husband lives under the headship of Christ is he able to channel into the family the mind and authority of Christ.

I once coached a football team, and early in the season I noticed something happening out on the field. There seemed to be confusion as the men walked up to the line and ran their plays. The word began to drift back to me in practice that everybody was offering his opinion in the huddle as to what play they should run. At that point I established headship. I told them that there was to be only one voice in the huddle—the voice of the quarterback. He was the man I was working with, and he was to call the plays. If anyone else talked in the huddle, the quarterback had authority to send him out of the game. The next game we ran the kickoff back to about the twenty-yard line. In the huddle the quarterback called the play, and it was the right play. He looked around and said, "Any objections?" No one said a word, and they went for a touchdown.

In this context headship functions simply to get a job done. No coach would say that the quarterback is more valuable than the end or more important than the halfback. All eleven men on the team are important. The quarterback simply has the *function* of headship in order that the team can move as a single unit.

One of the problems with the average family today is that there are too many captains! Everybody is pointing in a different direction. The wife has her idea, the kids have theirs, the husband has his idea, and they are all trying to run the ship in their own power and authority.

Christ chose to accomplish his will in the family through the principle of headship. He could have done it with a celestial loudspeaker. "All right down there at 1603 W. 7th Street! Time for morning devotions! Get up! Everybody on the ball!" But he has chosen to do it through headship. At 7:00 A.M. the husband calls the family together. "Time for morning devotions." That is just as much the voice and the will of God for that family as if it came from the heavenly loudspeaker. God has simply chosen to channel it through this principle of headship.

The world's idea of submission equates headship with superiority and submission with inferiority. That may be true in the world. Jesus said that the Gentiles lord it over those that are under them, but he also said that it should not be so among Christians. As a matter of fact, among Christians it is going to be almost the other way around. "He who is great among you shall be the servant of all." That is the stance the husband must take—not lording his authority over his family, but meekness and service.

The purpose of headship is to discover and express the will of God. It is not to inflict the will of the husband upon the family. If a husband is to speak for God, he first has to give up his own will. If he does that, then the spirit in which he approaches his wife is altogether different. He does not approach her as someone he has to convince or steamroll in order to get his way. Instead, he realizes that if he is responsible to get the mind of God then he needs to listen carefully to his wife because God may use her as a channel of revelation.

Some people think that headship means the husband has the last word. The husband, however, doesn't *have* the last word; he simply *speaks* the last word. As head of the family, he is responsible before God to discern the will of God for the family, and when he has discerned it as best he is able (having listened carefully to his wife, weighing her counsel, her fears and misgivings, her insight and judgment), then he *speaks* the last word. But *Christ has* the last word if that family is living in divine order. A family in which Christ has the last word includes a contented wife, blessed children, and a godly husband.

4

A New Look at Christian Wives

GLADYS M. HUNT

Just and honorable causes have their hazards. The sheer volume of words used to defend, ennoble, berate, define, propagandize, or otherwise raise consciousness often leaves a gray blur in the mind. And while this is no comment on the validity of the cause, it is an indication of the absolute necessity for incisive and biblical thinking, which is precisely where the hazard lies. Causes are disturbing, emotional, subjective, and confusing. Truth does not come in neatly tied packages labeled with formulas. It hangs out of the edges of our boxes and is sometimes hardly found inside the package at all. We struggle to stuff all the loose ends in so we can have a "system." We oversimplify; we weigh the evidence. Our rhetoric is often convincing; our experiences less so.

What is true of causes in general is certainly true of the feminist movement. Sometimes people ask, "What do you think of women's lib?" as if they were merely inquiring whether you liked wide lapels on men's suits. Who has a tidy answer for a question as big as that? *Where would you like to begin?* What is just and true, and what trappings have accumulated that are gross and detracting?

Within the Christian community the spectrum of thought on the

GLADYS HUNT has written many books, including *MS Means Myself*, and *The Christian Way of Death*. She has worked closely with her husband Keith in Inter-Varsity Christian Fellowship and is the author of a number of Bible study guides. The Hunts have one son and live in Ann Arbor, Michigan.

women's movement narrows to at least identifiable points of view. On one end of the spectrum are the more militant, liberal points of view, perhaps best represented by Alan Graebner in *After Eve* and Letha Scanzoni and Nancy Hardesty in *All We're Meant to Be.* Advocates of this point of view generally espouse egalitarian marriages and decry role identifications. Concepts of submission and headship are battlegrounds for fresh interpretations, and male/female differentiations are explained away as acculturation processes. They chafe under a patriarchal system which leads them to irritation with the fatherhood of God. They talk about "self-actualization" and "direct participation in the world" (whatever that means) which almost inevitably demands a career for the wife (so she has something interesting to talk about) and a division of labor in the home. Equality and subordination are labeled contradictions. The latter means servanthood, and that is not a popular idea.

Reacting on the other end of the spectrum (and often with much less careful thought) are the adherents to the submissive/manipulative techniques advocated by Marabel Morgan in *The Total Woman* and a number of books and courses like *Fascinating Womanhood* and *The Philosophy of Christian Womanhood.* Submission in this corner is almost the first tenet of the Christian faith. A woman must do what a man requires, and while the courses are generally directed toward wives, the underlying tone is that all women are submissive to all men. Far from being discouraged from role-playing, wives are encouraged to play roles of helplessness, childlikeness, and general opinionlessness to enhance the male ego. The basic premise which determines a woman's behavior is a needy male ego. (Make him feel big and strong and capable, and he will be!)

Morgan's emphasis on sex, designed to bring the husband straight home from work to see what new costume she might be wearing, is manipulative in nature rather than relational. Other courses overextend biblical submission to the point of excluding possibilities for genuine human relationships. While many have found help in the section on family life in *Basic Youth Conflicts* taught by Bill Gothard, his use of metaphors like chain-of-command, the hierarchy, the husband as hammer, the wife as chisel, and the child as stone to define family relationships is depersonalizing and makes room for unfortunate extremes in interpretation. And, as is so often the case, disciples push beyond masters in arriving at their positions.

The tangle is heightened when the disciples of submissiveness feel assuredly more spiritual and biblical than the advocates of a more liberal stance, while those questioning traditional biblical interpretations often feel more enlightened and liberated, and even of superior intellect. Feelings begin getting in the way of truth, and our individual interpretation of truth is colored by our experience, and our experience becomes our personal security blanket.

In a sense we are victims of a technical age in which answers are spit out of a computer, neatly defined on tape. And there is security in a tight system. We have to resist consciously the temptation to seek formulas that make life work and find safety in these rather than in the living God. It troubles me that in our attempts to find our way through the morass of abuse and hostility in our world, we are so often trapped by extreme positions which may be convincingly packaged but often indicate how little we understand about the nature of biblical truth, authentic, mature relationships, and our own humanity. We are selfish and we are pragmatic. We ask, Does it make me happy? and Does it work? The real question is, Is it truth?

In this milieu of contemporary thought about women we need to take a new look at Christian wives. We have been influenced, we are being influenced, and we shall be influenced in the days ahead. And that is not bad in itself; we want to grow, and we cannot grow without examining new ideas. But we are also *influencers,* and that makes critical thinking and careful decisions about larger values more necessary than ever before.

What is the *larger value* that is central to meaningful living? Is it not *quality relationships* that all of us long for? All about us marriages are disintegrating, even those we thought were stable and compatible. People, in a panic for happiness, look for it in new experiences rather than inside themselves. With callous ruthlessness men and women reject each other and their children. We have lost sight of the simplest truth—relationships make life worthwhile. In going back to the Book of Genesis to investigate the details of creation, we miss the point if we do not see this. In a profound sense, all truth is for relationship. It is human to relate, and God meant for truths about himself to be reflected in our relationships— truths about unity, goodness, mercy, faithfulness, steadfast love. Yet it is in the area of personal relationships that we suffer most acutely. We understand so little of the potential of our humanity and what constitutes quality relationships. We do not face our own basic needs. Therefore, we are prone to believe a lie.

The lie is simply that there is an easier way to handle our pain than to work on our capacity for genuine relationships. Relationships are hard going. Surely, we think, there must be an easier way to feel fulfilled, to realize our potential, to feel good about ourselves. The tragedy is that this attitude also may define our Christian lives. We want to be sure we are going to heaven (Tell me how I can be sure I'm saved!), but please don't ask us to live in dynamic relationship with God. That's too hard! And yet that is what God has called us to. We would prefer to manipulate God into responding as we think he should. Maintaining relationships does not fit our instamatic culture. I am deeply concerned lest formulas, techniques, and legitimate concerns about women deflect us from pressing on for what is good and excellent in our relationships.

That two persons could be open with each other, sharing deeply, transparent in the most intimate areas of life, forgiving each other, serving each other, transcending self to enhance and affirm each other—this quality relationship needs to be openly declared as that larger good that we seek in Christian marriage. This kind of beauty, this kind of fulfillment of our humanity makes a worthy goal for Christian wives. Nothing less will do.

This is also what makes home a safe place, not two people standing over against each other, trying to manipulate the other to please self, but two people standing beside each other and sharing life openly. Their embracing relationship is a fragrance of life, of faithfulness, of truth in a world of suspicion and anxiety. These two are not perfect, but they are a growing, loving, redeeming society, and what they are becoming is seen again in their children. Together they make a safe place in a fractured, cold world where others are warmed and encouraged by their love.

This is not some high-minded dream that lacks reality; it is coming to grips with the reality of redemption. When women have won all their rights and honor and equal opportunity, we will still face our emptiness if we have not worked out our human relationships. After we have tried all the new fads of practical manifestations of submissiveness, we will still have to face the needs of our own personhood and a deep urgency to experience quality oneness with another person. This is our basic need; its potential is found in the cross.

I would issue a new call to an old truth—a new call to Christian wives to maintain, to insist upon, to establish quality relationships in our lonely alienated world and to be satisfied with nothing less. We are recalled to our human potential, redeemed by God's grace. Three areas need fresh, wholesome emphasis to help us implement this goal: a high view of self, a high view of communication, and a high view of God.

A HIGH VIEW OF SELF

The issue here is not self-centeredness but selfhood. Every person needs to be convinced of his or her intrinsic worth, lest he or she spend life denying it or trying to prove it, both of which are wasteful and selfish. Life's pressures conspire to make us aware of all we are not, which leads us to the paralysis of comparison. We are extreme in our evaluations. If we are not certain things (clever, pretty, intelligent, aggressive), then we are probably nothing—a conclusion as shallow as the evidence we examine. Intrinsic means *belonging to a thing by its very nature.* We have been made in the image of God.

We sat around the dinner table one evening with a small circle of treasured friends, and in the safety of the love we shared, one woman opened her heart and said, "Do I exist just because my parents came together, or did God want *me*? Am I a mistake or a plan? And would it have mattered if I had never lived? I think if at my conception I had been given a vote, I would have voted no. Not because life has been so bad, but because I sometimes wonder if it matters, *really* matters that I am here."

She was sharing the inner heart of human beings. I thought of how many people over the centuries have thrown themselves on

the ground or across their beds and cried, "Do I matter, really
matter to anyone?" My friend is not a depressive; she is a well-put-
together woman who enters lovingly into the lives of others. In the
conversation that followed, our son offered the most penetrating
answer, "If you had never been born," he said, "you could never
know God."

We are born to know God, to relate to him, to experience his
friendship. We are twice his: by creation and by redemption. Our
worth is found in his heart; he thought we were worth dying for.
Our intrinsic worth can only be understood as we see God's love
and mercy toward us.

Hagar must have felt that way. She was a slave, bearing a child
for her master, then being sent away because of jealousy—used,
abused, desperate, deserted. And then the voice of God from
heaven, "What troubles you, Hagar? Fear not, for God . . ." We
are not dispensable to God. We are unworthy, but we are not
worthless. God has proven all that needs to be proven about us.
Unless we believe this and begin to work it into the stuff of our
being, we will be caught up in self-absorption and never be free
to move out into the lives of others in any meaningful way. We
will look instead for hundreds of other ways to feel good about
ourselves, and none of them will be as validating as worth found
in the heart of God. It is basically a spiritual transaction; it involves
believing, *accepting*, and *experiencing* God's love.

If it is that easy, you may say, why is the world so filled with
self-centered people? It is *not* easy. That is why no formula can be
given, only principles of truth. Each person works out this concept
of selfhood in the individuality of his or her own experience. We
are each a complex bundle of past encounters; we have picked up
vibrations about ourselves from our family relationships, some positive and some negative. Experiencing human love does make it
easier to believe that God loves us, and those who have suffered
this kind of deprivation often have a wall of bitterness that shuts
others out. The elements of affirmation and acceptance from others
are critical in the communication of God's love. He does not place
us in a vacuum.

Yet there is a loving God, infinitely creative and personal, who
wants to get through to us. I am sometimes staggered by our
human rigidity—that meeting love, we would refuse it. People

so often refuse love from God and others. A declaration of love is nothing to a person who does not accept it. I know women whose fathers rejected them and who are spoiling their lives by placing that anger onto their husbands and refusing to love or to receive love. They are intelligent, achieving women who have accurate insights into their reactions and have stopped right there, wasting years in resentment and refusing happiness. One mother confessed to me that as a young girl her sense of rejection peaked one night when she wanted to sit on her mother's lap and was pushed away. Now married and four children later, she has refused her lap to her own children and warm affection to her husband, still trying to punish her mother for hurting her.

Out of such prisons and other small places God wants to deliver us. He is willing, able, eager. What he waits for is openness on our part. How whole we are depends in large measure on the risks we will take in letting go of self-absorption to let God bring us into selfhood.

That is basic, but there is more. Selfhood involves accepting the responsibility to be your own unique self in the world, not someone else's expectation of you. Only persons can relate, not projections of another person, not masks, not pretenders. Looking at an occasional marriage I have thought that the likelihood of a good relationship was slim simply because the wife's sense of selfhood was missing. She did not bring her uniqueness to the relationship, only a sense of vague humanity without conviction or assured expression of personality. Unless she grew, she would later exert little positive influence in her home.

Good relationships come out of a deep sense of personhood on the part of both people in the relationship. Nothing is more misleading than a view of oneness that reduces two people to an amalgamated blob, in which both persons lose their identity. A blob cannot relate. It takes two persons to relate, and oneness emerges out of the refinement of their communication. We have the example of the unity within the Godhead in this. The Father, the Son, and the Holy Spirit are distinct personalities who are perfect oneness. Oneness is not sameness or nothingness.

I stress this because of the large number of wives who submerge themselves in the lives of others, not out of health, but out of personal fear. It is a good thing to be John's wife and Susan's and

Tom's mother, but if this is all that defines you in your own mind, who will you be if something happens to John and when Susan and Tom leave home?

Because relationships are our goal, our expression of selfhood is not destructive to other people. The kind of "right to be myself" that cheats or mars others is mistaken identity, and persons who are experiencing genuine selfhood are sensitive in such expressions. No one belongs to himself or to herself; there is no such thing as autonomy, whether married or single. As a wife, there are some things I said no to when I said yes to my husband. (And he did the same. It's called love.)

People who experience a sense of selfhood are growing people who let others grow. Increasingly, threats that make us protest and protect our self are no longer threats. We can let other people be who they are because we are becoming who we are. We dare to try new adventures and learn new skills. Neither failure nor success changes our basic worth.

A high view of selfhood means a high view of womanhood. That's a given. Sexuality is not incidental, but purposive. It is deeply rooted in our humanity. As women we have only one way to express ourselves in the world—as persons who are created female. Accepting selfhood for women means accepting womanhood. There are some obvious physical limitations inherent in being female, and to deny these is simply foolishness. To accept or enjoy them is more natural. In other areas, restrictions placed on women need to be examined with freshness and integrity. We cannot continue to carry around antiquated, emotional concepts without thinking them through. It is part of accepting the responsibility for selfhood.

A growing sense of selfhood is the prerequisite to quality relationships. No one sits in isolation waiting to emerge a fully developed self. Each of these growth processes are simultaneous and contingent on one another. We come to know ourselves as we relate to others.

A HIGH VIEW OF COMMUNICATION

We also need a high view of communication, which is the same as a high view of others. It may seem a strange tack to discuss communication with wives who are traditionally considered as liking to talk, when it is they who most often complain about husbands who won't talk. But talking and genuine communication are not the same. Thoreau said that it takes two to speak a truth—one to speak and another to listen. The burden of genuine communication is on the listener. Listening is more than openness; it is a desire to come face to face with the other person's thoughts. Good listening makes for good communication. Paul Tillich once said, "The first duty of love is to listen."

Communication is the heart of quality relationships, for it means getting into significant touch with the other person. The very being of one is open to the very being of the other. It is mutual self-disclosure. Two people come close to each other at the most intimate level of their being and share. Tournier writes of this:

> It is the sudden flash of honesty, the moment of transparency, which overwhelms us and transfigures the climate of our relationships with other people. There is no such thing as complete transparency. There is only one supremely privileged relationship in which we approach anywhere near it, and that is marriage. That is what imparts to marriage, when it is a true dialogue, its incomparable richness, its prodigious capacity for developing the person and showing us ourselves as we really are.[1]

Communication is a way of saying I love you.

Not all self-disclosure is honest; it is possible to disclose a false self. Self-disclosure must be honest if a quality relationship is to develop. That is why there is no room in quality relationships for the kind of manipulation that makes a game out of human relationships. All the moves are set up for the payoff. Marked by duplicity and pretense, such events are not a true encounter of persons who seek deep intimacy. Ultimately such game playing only makes us aware that the world is full of schemes, deceptions, and inauthenticity and that even our homes are unsafe.

Sexual game playing is perhaps the most disillusioning, for it cheapens and mocks the true expression of oneness. Meaningful sex is the joyous celebration of meaningful relationships of total people who are totally committed to each other. It involves abandoning self in a way that leaves the partners extremely vulnerable. It is only a matter of time before one or another of them comes to realize that games do not make true relationships and that more than bodies need to be shared if there is to be quality communication. This is a call for Christian wives to recognize in a fresh way what makes for genuine relationship and not to toy with gimmicks which degrade its value.

But can a person demand this kind of communication and transparency of relationship? We cannot *demand* anything in human relationships. That would be like demanding that someone love us. But we can have a goal; we can talk together about a goal larger than our individual selves; we can dream together about that big thing we want to build out of our marriage. We cannot demand, but we can create an environment, and we can persist in prayer and in our willingness to be known. It takes self-disclosure to invite self-disclosure. The insistence to bring this about is not to satisfy *me;* it is to build *us.*

The wife who persists in asking, "What are you thinking?" probably will never find out. Surely God can make us more aware and creative than that, and he can control any obsession for overkill in communication. We need to learn to listen to what has already been said. Quality communication does not mean sharing every thought and feeling of the day; it means safety to share one's very self.

> Communication is a willingness to know and be known. It is two-directional, the communicator first being able to accept himself, then willing to communicate that self. Communication between marriage partners requires that they both rise to the plane of honesty and open-heartedness in everything. And what does this mean but the need for a large measure of God's grace and enablement? It takes humility, which only the Lord can give, if such openness and honesty is to prevail.[2]

Communication of this kind is a risk. Intimacy is always costly, but lack of it is more costly. We hold other people's lives in trust. We must learn to communicate, and we must encourage it in those we love. Self-disclosure and listening are keys; integrity is the watchword.

But, you say, do you know the reality of so many relationships?

Some men have only wanted a second mother, not a wife to share their life. Others are possessive and domineering because they can't bear the thought of not being right or top man in the kingdom. Some want a nonthreatening alter ego and don't expect much spiritually or intellectually from their wives. Other husbands have built a totally separate life and are essentially nonsharers. Some want their wives to be only a pretty, sexy possession.

Yes, everyone has noticed this. (And there is the other side to the coin, too.) But how did this state of being come about between Christians under the lordship of Christ? That these things are tolerated in Christian marriage is an affront to the example of our Lord Jesus Christ and to his work on the cross. Could it be because Christian wives themselves have had too little understanding of the potential of human relationships and have been too self-centered? What have we been talking about together all these years?

To react as a chafing wife who shouts, "I'm a person, too" (which is assuredly true!), is not to reach the goal either. Neither will the cheated wife's "I want my turn, too" win the prize. Just causes are often ruined by personal sinfulness.

Somehow we have come to accept a standing over against each other instead of a standing together. It is difficult to tell how much of this comes from a faulty understanding of what constitutes biblical submission. Certainly submission is no ground for a kind of tyranny on the husband's part that shuts off the possibilities of the quality life we have been talking about. God never condones behavior based on superego needs. Jesus Christ, the perfect demonstration of human potential, said, "I am among you as one who serves." Some teaching about submission has been fertile soil in which uncrucified flesh prospers.

Submission is not a game a woman plays to get the upper hand. Some who give the most ready appearance of submissiveness have in fact become master manipulators. This kind of thinking was illustrated in a *Christianity Today* (July 20, 1973) interview with Kathryn Kuhlman. She commented, "When it comes to women's lib, I am still as old-fashioned as the Word of God. I still think the husband should be the head of the family. I know how it was at our house. If Papa said it, it was as though God had said it.

We never had any women's lib, but we had a mighty happy family. Papa did the work, and Mama ran Papa without Papa knowing it, and it was a beautiful situation." If her perception of the situation is correct, this is anything but a beautiful situation.

Nothing in the headship of the husband hints that he has the infallibility of God, but if he did, the horror of running such a person without his knowing it needs to strike home. We tragically give the same kind of lip-service to the lordship of Christ. Yes, he is our Lord. Then we manipulate all the situations and do our own thing.

Neither of these concepts of submission allows the quality relationships we have been discussing. Submission *is* a biblical idea. God has never liked arrogance or self-centeredness. The teaching of Scripture emphasizes humility as that which pleases God, and Jesus himself spoke of being "meek and lowly of heart." The specific teaching about submission within marriage begins with Ephesians 5:21 where all believers are instructed about relationships, "Be subject to one another out of reverence for Christ." Wives are a specific example of what is required of all Christians; they are to be submissive to their husbands. But the person to whom I submit is my lover, not an enemy, an ogre, or a tyrant. And my lover is to love like Christ. In the end, what is submission but sacrificial self-giving, and what is love but sacrificial self-giving? The wife's submission emphasizes the husband's responsibility as head, but in the end both are demonstrating that Ephesians 5:21 works in relationships because of the new life style of those who know Jesus Christ.

Personally, biblical authority and my own common sense warn me against wriggling out from under the teaching of the headship of the husband, as if all my freedom and fulfillment depended on being my own head. Paul states that headship is rooted in creation, and as such the husband's authority is given him by God. But how is he to use that authority? The instruction is not, "Be authoritative," but, "Love your wives." The emphasis is on responsibility, and the husband's authority is seen in his enhancing, serving, giving life style. Both husband and wife are responsible to God, and their responsibilities are two aspects of the same thing. Biblical submission does not spoil quality relationships; our failure is found in the sinfulness that sets us against each other and in our low appropriation of the grace of our Lord Jesus Christ.

A HIGH VIEW OF GOD

I believe Christian wives are called to a high view of God. This is not last in order of importance, but obviously present throughout the discussion. What we believe about God is the most important thing about us. It will be evidenced in all our choices and decisions, in the way we handle our problems, and in the resources we choose to furnish our lives.

A Christian has a living relationship with the living God. Maintaining our part in the relationship will be our largest adventure in growing. We will have encounters with this living God who acts in our personal history, who longs to tell us who we are, who answers our prayers, and who pulls us up to his standard as we walk with him. It's no mean adventure to know God.

But as in all relationships, the quality of our life with God depends on our willingness to know and be known. God has consistently taken the initiative in making himself known. As James Packer says so beautifully, "As one listens to what the Bible says he comes to realize that God is actually opening his heart to him, making friends with him, enlisting him as a colleague . . . to be His fellow-worker and personal friend."[3] In our love relationship with the living God we listen, we respond, we communicate, and we experience his fellowship in our lives. *Know* is a grace word. It is more than an intellectual exercise. The Bible says Adam *knew* his wife, a euphemism for sexual intercourse. In the same way, knowledge of God cannot be divorced from personal encounter and personal intimacy. "God is not a theorem; He is a person. As such, He is only known and encountered in a total relationship which involves and affects not only the mind, but the life and character as well. To know His dossier is nothing; to know Him is everything."[4]

A high view of God gives us an inner discipline to know him, and the fruit of that knowledge changes our human condition. He makes us firm and persistent; he makes us warm-hearted and accepting; he teaches us how to love by the overflow of the love he pours into our hearts. He gives us large tasks and great fulfillments. He is in the business of affirming and enhancing all of his children. As we come close to him, we feel safer in all our other relationships.

We are Christians. We dare not be obscurantists, refusing to face contemporary cultural issues. We need to grapple with all the hard questions and use discernment to sort out truth. We need personal integrity in our own emotional life.

But what the world needs most of all is not answer-people, but *models.* People are looking for examples, for life styles that demonstrate love, harmony, quality relationships. Far too many have forgotten the possibilities of human relationships, if indeed they ever knew they existed. We need to make our maximum contribution where it will most affect the declining quality of family life and marriage relationships. As we find our way personally in defining selfhood, in refining our communication, and in pressing on to know the Lord, we *can* influence others in establishing quality relationships. I believe the world is asking, "Come, show us how to live. Show us how the gospel works in your closest relationships. Show us what it means to belong to each other."

We need to turn the tide away from emotional nonsupport to a flood of evidence that in Christ walls are broken down and people can relate. God pours his love into our hearts by the Holy Spirit whom he has given us (Rom. 5:5). In our homes there should be an excess of love that runs out the door and flows down the street to meet the needs of others and is a model for human relationships.

NOTES

1. Paul Tournier, *The Meaning of Persons,* trans. Edwin Hudson (New York: Harper & Row, 1957), p. 135.

2. Dwight Hervey Small, *After You've Said I Do* (Westwood, N.J.: Fleming H. Revell, 1968), p. 67.

3. James I. Packer, *Knowing God* (Downers Grove, Ill.: Inter-Varsity Press, 1973), p. 32.

4. R. T. France, *The Living God* (Downers Grove, Ill.: Inter-Varsity Press, 1970), p. 55.

5

Reasons Marriages Fail— Communication

MARK W. LEE

The problems of a failing marriage may be related to unsatisfactory communication. Failure in interpersonal communication ranks high on lists of complaints in faulty marriages. Some analysts contend that this failure is the *primary* cause for unhappiness among family members.

We should become aware that members of a family wish to communicate and not communicate at the same time. This ambivalence is strong. A spouse will demand communication with his mate on some subject. After short discussion, he may say, "I don't want to talk about it." In some situations resistance comes from intimidation; in others, resistance is the result of being bested in an argument. But there are cases in which parties seek communication at the same time as there arises within them resistance to it. Resistance tends to win the internal competition. Communication loses.

A summary of communication ideas and transactional analysis is appropriate background material. This analysis may explain part of

MARK W. LEE is the president of Simpson College in San Francisco. Previously he taught speech and communication at Whitworth College, Spokane, and Northwestern College, Minneapolis. He is a member of the Speech Association of America, and is a consultant in management and communication for several organizations including Standard Oil of Virginia. He is the author of *Our Children: Our Best Friends,* and his *Why Marriages Fail* is to be published soon. Dr. Lee is married and has four children and three grandchildren.

the communication insecurity persons feel, even the failure of communication between devoted family members. The widely circulated book *I'm OK—You're OK* by Thomas Harris is a leading transactional resource.[1] Harris wrote about three influential orientations in every human being—the parent, the child, and the adult. The parent influence tends to be autocratic, the child emotional, and the adult rational. Each of these emerges to greater or lesser degrees in life experiences, and the secret of effective and responsible living is to permit the control of one's own "adult" to emerge. Harris argued that one may recognize which attitude—parent, child, or adult—"is originating each stimulus and response." Marriages are greatly influenced by these emerging attitudes. Both verbal and nonverbal clues tend to reveal the state of the individual, as Harris shows:

Parent Clues—Physical: Furrowed brow, pursed lips, the pointing index finger, head wagging . . .

Parent Clues—Verbal: I am going to put a stop to this *once and for all;* I can't for the life of me . . . ; Now always remember . . . ; How many times have I told you? . . . ; If I were you . . .

Child Clues—Physical: . . . tears, the quivering lip; pouting; temper tantrums; the high-pitched, whining voice; . . . giggling . . .

Child Clues—Verbal: . . . I wish, I want, I dunno . . . I guess . . .

Adult Clues—Physical: . . . the Adult is identified by continual movement—of the face, the eyes, the body. . . . Non-movement signifies non-listening . . .

Adult Clues—Verbal: . . . the basic vocabulary of the Adult consists of why, what, where, when, who and how . . . how much, in what way, comparative, true, false, probable, possible, unknown, objective, I think, I see . . .

Harris discusses some of the communication problems which plague a family. A father may fall into the habit of talking like a parent (autocratic) to everyone in the family. His wife may find this approach objectionable and complain. His older children resist him. Or a mother may talk like a child (emotional) to her husband and children. She will lose some of the force of her ideas.

The Harris material above utilizes a major concept in communication: Verbal and nonverbal elements are present and influential in interpersonal relationships. Receivers (listeners and readers) as well as senders (speakers or writers) interpret various clues in communication to determine meanings, values, feelings, and attitudes. In addition, time, place, and circumstances are important to the success of any communication. The purpose of this chapter is to discuss verbal, nonverbal, and environmental factors in marriage communications.

MARITAL PROBLEMS AND VERBAL COMMUNICATION

Marital problems may be related to unsatisfactory verbal communication. Common problem areas occur in the choice of words, word groupings, and ideas used in conversations among family members. Relative to the choice of words, several are particularly troublesome:

Inflammatory words. These are sometimes called "gunpowder" words. When used, they almost immediately distress a mate and arouse anger. They are sometimes deliberately chosen for the purpose of precipitating domestic tension. Family members may use communication to create misunderstanding, which is contrary to the right purpose of language. To use words which would negatively affect wife or husband or child suggests immaturity in the communicator. Some persons create tension as a way of life by the words they use. Word choices are not accidental in this sense although the originator is not likely aware of the full impact of his conduct, either on himself or on the victim of his procedure. Lack of empathy by a mate is a common complaint in marital counseling: "He knows I am angered when he says those things, but he says them anyway." If his wife does not wish to hear a term or be called a name, why would the husband use the word, even if he believed it to be affectionate?

Withheld words. These are unspoken words which ought to have been spoken. When a person deliberately withholds words of comfort or understanding, or when he offers silent treatment, he is as guilty of wrong action as if he had fiercely argued. Withheld words, at the least, create doubt through silence. To know that one wishes to hear some word of love, comfort, or admission ought to be enough to inspire the appropriate response, but the usefulness of response is not always recognized. Wives sometimes address their husbands but receive no response in word, though the husbands will, by doing the chores requested, reveal they heard the petition. A word as well as compliance from the husband would provide a human and loving experience. If a woman wishes a response from her husband, she can usually extract it by calling his name, awaiting or compelling a response, and then stating the idea. A friend once complained that her husband would come to dinner when called but did not orally acknowledge her invitation. She was assured that she could get an answer, utilizing the technique of calling his name, awaiting his reply, and then stating her interest. That evening she tried it successfully. She learned that the greatest responsibility for the success of a communication rested with the sender. The sender, if skilled, can likely evoke a self-gratifying response.

Discouraging words. These are generally attempts to diminish a person, or concept, or achievement. They may steal emotional life from otherwise expectant and adventuresome persons. Especially may they do so when directed to children. Examples of discouraging words are: "You never do anything right," "You may not be pretty, but beauty isn't everything," "Anybody could have done what you did." Such statements diminish recognition, balance, and enthusiasm. They disregard the human need for confidence building.

Gossipy words. These are meant to demean persons. They are not supported by evidence and may be lies. Almost always they create distortions. At best, they introduce shallow insights, but like all devious approaches they will, if sustained in practice, warp something of the personality of the one who originates or entertains them. Some examples of gossipy words are: "Well, you know what they say about you," "I suppose your attitudes are recognized by the people in the church," "You can be suspicious of him because of his friends—birds of a feather flock together," "I wonder what's wrong with him—no women friends." Gossip is weakened when the one gossiped about refuses to dignify what is said. Gossip tends to die when it is disregarded.

Angle words. These are utilized as a devious technique. One person approaches another with a sideswipe. Rather than tell his wife that he would like to see her better groomed, the man states, "Boy, Joyce sure looked nice today. Her hair was well done, and she wore a beautiful dress." It would be far better if the man could suggest, with caution, some things his wife might do to improve her appearance. His wife well knows that Joyce is always attractive, always well groomed. The remark is cowardly. Instead of shaming his wife into improving herself, the husband may arouse bitterness and anger, even jealousy. Why is her husband so interested in Joyce?

Laughing words. These words seem to be said jokingly, but no joke is intended. The person is serious and uses the cruelty of humor to hammer down mate or child. For example: "It was great fun watching you try to get into that car. The doors must be too small." If the person is overweight and sensitive about it, to joke about the size of doors is not a means for improving relationships or reducing sensitivity about the subject. A man had a penchant for hurting his wife and others with his "laughing remarks." It appeared that his pseudohumor was a means for suppressing his own sense of inadequacy. When others used a similar style of conversation at his expense, he felt ill-treated. Gradually he changed and mellowed, becoming sensitive to his wife.

Question words. These words are not used to ask questions but to interpret and accuse. Very likely the person talking, if challenged, would claim to have asked for information, but the voice inflection proves otherwise. "How stupid can you get?" "Are you going to straighten the matter out or aren't you?" "What do you think I am, a moneybags or something?" If these qualify as questions, they are the lowest form.

In husband-wife relationships the judgmental question is commonly used by the wife. She employs it as a weapon and sometimes perceives it as her only verbal defense. It does not present her case very well. Generally, the approach prejudices her rightful complaints. She seems to be overreacting and may give an impression of rebellion and self-persecution. Often the questions will be introduced in the body of a statement which the husband is trying to make: "Have you ever been concerned with my needs?" "Do you ever go where I want to go?" "Are you interested in anyone besides yourself?"

Pronoun words. These words depersonalize wife or husband or child. The tendency to use the pronouns *he* or *she* or *his* or *hers* may indicate a decayed relationship. Happy couples commonly use the plural pronoun *we* or *our* and endearing words to address each other. As one writer put the idea, "Don't let the 'we-ness' go out of your marriage." There is a difference between, "He goes his way and I go mine," and, "We have learned that we enjoy working at separate projects." The two express similar facts about conduct but different feelings about the attitudes of the couple. The use of pronouns, like the use of other parts of speech, is often unconscious. Counselors discover unrecognized negative attitudes through this clue.

Contradictory words. These words propound a contrary position as a matter of habit. This pattern introduces a psychological aggression which provides an illusion of superiority for the contradicting person. For example: "She always says that, but she is wrong, as anyone who has studied the subject knows." "He wants to go on Friday, but Saturday is better." "I think the children should have more freedom, but she holds them down."

We are not sure why many persons always wish to take a contrary position. No subject is so inconsequential but that they are unwilling to permit it to pass. Contradictions of this character are common barriers to communication. We dislike talking to persons who create the atmosphere of competition through the challenge of unimportant details. Perhaps most of us have been embarrassed to engage in conversation in which husband or wife in remark after remark corrects some minor statement or detail of the other: "It wasn't the fifth, it was the sixth." "They didn't go to Oregon, it was Washington." If the fact were vital to the context of the conversation, then the correction should be welcomed. The issue here relates only to relatively inconsequential details.

Repetitious words. These words "rub it in." Dissatisfied with making a point, the person psychologically pushes and presses others for personal gratification. One may say, "I told you, I told you, I told you." The threefold accent represents more than an idea. It reveals emotional irritation and an illusion of superiority. The repetition then becomes the emotional reason for rejecting the truth that a warning had been issued or that failure would follow that action. Economy of words by the sender is a commendable practice when failure and embarrassment have occurred for the listener.

Identification with one's mate rather than segregation from him is evidence of love and human insight. The problem and its revelation referred to above would provide an excellent situation for the use of the plural pronoun, "Well, we missed it this time. Can we find something meaningful in the event?"

Profane words. These are commonly called the "four-letter" words and are sometimes used by Christians of one another. A few years ago it would not have been presumed that this category of language would appear in any prose aimed at dedicated Christians. Even in some Christian homes there may now be heard, harshly spoken, "Go to hell," "I don't give a damn," or "He's a bastard." None of these, when used by troubled couples, have contributed to solutions in any instance of counseling in which I have engaged. It is common knowledge that language does change, and wise men do not force either their own meanings upon symbols or insist on language purity. In any event, they will not get purity. Strong words do become weak, and weak strong. Words may and do change their meanings, sometimes totally. However, there are words representing concepts which are not easily stated except as traditionally they have been stated. When a mate is serious and intense in conversation, he may find little essential change in the meaning of *damn* or *hell* from that which was meant by his forefathers in similar conversations. The large difference is that Christian forefathers would not likely use words of this nature with members of their families. And there is a logic which denies their use. What is the meaning of such words in conversation? Are they contrived to heal or to comfort? Really, what is their value? If they are no longer severe, what words have been coined to express the severity they once represented?[2]

Egotistical words. These words imply the wisdom of one partner and the stupidity of the other. The most common phrase in this group is, "I told you so." There is also, "If you would only follow my advice." Nebuchadnezzar lost his advantage before God when he said proudly, "Is not this great Babylon which I have built?" And the king of the house will lose some respect of his queen when he takes the ego route. The problem here commonly belongs to the male. His work takes him into a world of commerce and activity which is considerably more varied than the environment of a home where the conversation is somewhat limited for a wife who is busy rearing preschool youngsters. A woman complained, "He expects me to understand what he understands; do with ease what he is able to do. How can I, when my whole day's conversation is at the depth of our three-year-old?"

Absolutes are identified with egotistical words. Learn the value of ending the use of absolutes with each other. Avoid the use of words like *always* or *never*. A helpful motto is: "Never use never." Paul Rees counseled on the issue: "Be sparing in the use of 'never.' It has ruined many a marriage." Rees noted how troubled couples may use sentences like, "You *never* show any appreciation," "You *never* clean up the bathroom after you shave," "You *never* say whether you like my hat or not," "You *never* have my breakfast on time," "You're *never* home when I call from the office."

The above list makes up what may be called "the dirty dozen" in verbal communication problems in marriage. But there are other communication barriers, generally caused by nonverbal clues, which may be even more serious. Add them to the wrong words, and conversation almost certainly fails. When it does, marriage seems cold and sterile.

Style problems occur when the combination of words is wrong, when the choice of the words and the way they are combined create ill feeling or place undue emotional meaning to a statement. Nearly every topic may be treated in three ways—crude, pedestrian, or sophisticated. The care in choosing the level of language will determine to a great extent success or failure with a person. The belief of many counselors and psychiatrists that a person is not free until he can use the "low brow" or "gutter" words is a claim which is not supportable, and there is much to be said against it. The most important thing to remember relative to this matter of style is to give as much advanced thought as possible to ideas which, when stated poorly, easily arouse misunderstandings and tensions. When stated well, those ideas are, at the least, not poisoned by poorly chosen words which arouse negative emotions.[3]

Meanings are easily distorted when the speaker or listener does not place himself in the position of the other person—does not "live in his skin." This is sometimes related to the "semantic problem" which presumes that when something has been said there is understanding and clarity on the part of the listener. It is important for talkers to assume that they are going to be misunderstood. That assumption will make one more patient in explanation and more tolerant of the people to whom he speaks. If, after making a statement of consequence, the talker asks the listener to repeat what he has heard, a recital likely will be returned which is not wholly satisfactory. The speaker responds, "That is not what I meant." Carl Rogers, the eminent psychologist, has proposed that a listener should reproduce the speaker's message to the speaker's satisfaction in order to qualify as an effective listener. Listening is vital to effective communication, and listeners take too little responsibility for their part in the communication cycle. In seeming contradiction of the foregoing references to the duty of the sender of a message, the listener or receiver may function ineffectively to a degree that no matter how well a message is transmitted the presumed receiver will fail to pick it up.

The semantic problem is universal in communications situations but appears intensely troublesome in a marriage. Something is said based on a meaning in the mind of the sender, whereas the receiver attributes his own meaning to the words picked up by his ear. The receiver then credits or blames the sender for the aroused thought. The sender generally has no mental image of the alternate concept which his words created in the listener's mind. But the listener presumes his perception is that of the speaker. In fact, it seldom, if ever, is the same. Although he may be almost entirely responsible for attributing foreign and extraneous meanings to the words of another, the listener seldom thinks of blaming himself.

This wholly human situation may be further aggravated. Sensitive persons commonly twist words and impressions. They make false accusations and attribute wrong motives to communication senders. All persons become more or less victimized by the semantic problem. They readily recognize the error in others but not in themselves. Humorous situation comedies appearing on television, stage, and film take advantage of this common insight, the ability to recognize the human condition in everyone but ourselves. I know communication experts who communicate poorly in their own marriages.

Our best hope is to reduce the number of times such misunderstandings are generated and to understand what is happening. The easiest technique to remember, but a difficult one to apply, is *the question method*. This is not the accusative questions discussed and deplored earlier, but it is the sincere attempt to find out the truth of a matter. Appropriate questions will corroborate our impressions about half the time. Asking a question permits us to withdraw with dignity when we discover our unspoken opinion is wrong. Of all communication helps, none is more useful than sincere and seeking questions, gently spoken.

One additional suggestion which should prove helpful is the application of assumed good will. Seldom does a person mean deliberately to offend another. When he does offend on purpose, he may have serious personal problems which need attention. He may need assistance more than criticism. Most persons are offended by their own imaginations. They read in meanings which were unknown to the sender. They distort and twist words and attitudes. If I assume that persons (including mate and children) mean well, I will withhold anger and misunderstanding. I dare not take myself too seriously; I must keep an appropriate sense of humor. I refuse to believe that anyone, especially a member of my family, is out to hurt me, to get me, to embarrass me. In that spirit one is free, open, and teachable.[4]

MARITAL PROBLEMS AND NONVERBAL COMMUNICATION

Our interpretations of nonverbal signals (voice and gesture) are more accurate than interpretations of verbal signals or symbols (words). Many of us are word-centered persons. We attribute all power to words when, in face-to-face conversation, other factors are generally more important. Some authorities contend that the tone of voice, the facial gesture, and other variables are more vital than words in expressing feelings and aid vitally in interpreting ideas expressed by words. Often in a counseling session a wife will repeat statements her husband made which not only offended her but revealed his "true" feeling on an issue. When asked what tone of voice he used and what meanings *he* attached to the words, she was unsure. But she was sure of the meanings she gave to his statements at the time, and that is what she holds him responsible for. Something about the whole situation provided her with a conviction about his words. Words are important, but we have learned that they are inexact. To force a single meaning on a word or statement which is strictly my own is naïve and unjustified. It is unlikely that any substantive statement is seen in quite the same way by any two auditors. If a range of differences may occur with statements which have been guardedly constructed, how much greater the chance of misunderstanding between two persons who speak casually and without considered reflection.

Marital problems may grow out of unsatisfactory nonverbal communications. Vocal variables are important carriers of meaning. We interpret the sound of a voice, both consciously and subconsciously. We usually can tell, or feel we can, by voice pitch, rate, loudness, and quality the emotional meanings of the speaker. We can tell the sincerity or insincerity, the conviction or lack of conviction, the truth or falsity, and the like of most statements we hear. When a voice is raised in volume and pitch, the words will not convey the same meaning as when spoken softly in a lower register. The high and loud voice, with speeded rate and harsh quality, will likely communicate such a degree of emotion that the verbal message is greatly obscured, if not obliterated. The *manner* in which a message is delivered, which is nonverbal, is registered most readily by the listener. It may or may not be remembered for recall. However, the communicator tends to recall what he said rather than the manner of his speech.

Considerable research has been done in nonverbal communication. Some researchers claim that as much as 93 percent of interpersonal communication in America is nonverbal. If true, the actual effectiveness of words in a message would be 7 percent. Gerard Nierenberg, a New York City attorney, offered the lowest percentage of all writers for nonverbal elements in a communication. He contended that 20 to 25 percent of oral communication is nonverbal and that persons tend to receive only 40 percent of that.[5] Although the contradictions in statistics are significant, students in the field agree that nonverbal elements in communication are very important and need to be understood.

Loudness. The volume used should meet the needs of the persons who listen to the speaker. Each should speak loudly enough to be heard and to provide animation, variety, and emphasis. If one is too soft, he will be asked to repeat. When one must repeat often in a conversation, he declines in his own perception of his effectiveness, he loses conviction and will be interpreted less positively than should be the case. Feedback from the listener ought to be instructive to a humanly sensitive mate or parent. It is known that family members become slovenly in their speech with one another. They will accuse each other of losing their hearing or not paying attention.

For many homes, the problem is not softness but loudness. The decibel rate is high and tranquillity is unknown. A family can create an atmosphere by shouting so that no one takes anything seriously unless it is shouted. Children from homes in which the parents shout at one another or to the children show real problems in adjustment of their roles in building their own families. Called a number of times to dinner, a lad dropped his toys casually and headed for home when the level of his mother's voice reached that which he interpreted as meaningful. He said to his playmate, "There's mom at the *scream* door again!"

But there are others who, with good argument or poor, go at the business of conversation with such gusto that they seem always to be embroiled in argument. Counseling case histories repeat the stories of gentle men and women married to mates reared in homes which were always loud in conversational exchanges. The cultural differences were not recognized. Emotional and personal meanings were attributed to the patterns of each mate. The soft-spoken person interpreted the loud as chronically out of temper. The loud interpreted the soft-spoken as diffident and cold, even unloving. Loudness may be a sign of anger, but it may be evidence of a learned family life style. Softness may be disinterest but alternately may reveal a habit of expression.

Rate. Although the human ear can register meaningfully a much faster rate than any person uses, there is a habitual approach used by each person to which listeners become acclimated, and a mate or child is generally accepted with his established rate. Changes for faster or slower rates on specific occasions generally reveal some feeling of fear, judgmentalism, excitement, emphasis, or the like, which may or may not cause us to communicate well with those we love. Slowness in speech is an evidence of a bore.

Mates may bore one another simply by dragging out statements which could be made and terminated with fewer words and faster delivery. Bores are not generally on the wrong subjects so much as reviewing them in unacceptable delivery patterns. This is not to deny that subjects may be shallow, tedious, or the like, which make them boring to discuss.

The other end of the rate pattern is the glib, nonstop talker who is boring, not because of the rapidity of the speech, but because the material is not worthy of the production. The talker seems to rattle. Eloquent persons are distinguished from glib talkers because they, the eloquent, have something to say that is worth hearing.

Pitch. Women tend to encounter more problems with higher pitches than men. This is partly because women begin with higher-pitched voices. High pitches are commonly interpreted, by men and women in America, as communicative of unloving and immature emotional states. The more intense the emotion becomes or seems to become as represented in a voice, the less seriously are the words taken by a listener. For several years my wife's voice tended to rise in serious discipline situations with the children as emotions were aroused. After detecting a point on the scale of her pitches, the children would no longer hear what their mother said, hence disregarded content for an interpretation of emotion. She was talked into avoiding discussion with our young sons during certain tension-producing disciplinary periods so as not to lose their respect for her wisdom and authority. One son later thanked his mother for the decision. He had observed a friend lose contact with his mother because of this issue. The mother appeared to be out of emotional control because of her high-pitched voice. Her counsel, appropriate in concept, was lost in communication. She seemed to be whining at her children. They bristled at the sound of her voice.

Quality. Although the essential quality of a voice is set and remains unchanged, the human ear can detect small nuances which reveal feeling and interpretation. A person's voice quality may inspire or repulse those, including mate and children, who hear him or her. What may be taken as appropriate in one environment, a coach shouting at players, for example, may be inappropriate in another. The players perceive the practice of the coach as leadership.

Others, including family members, may actually tremble at the sound of his gruff and thunderous voice. Even in counseling sessions one may observe a man "tune out" his wife because of the shrewish impression she gives with her voice. Voices which seem objectionable are metallic, harsh, breathy, flat, muffled, and thin. The offenses caused by voice quality may create continuing problems for members of families. And persons are sometimes offended at the accents of their mates—foreign or regional American.

Physical variables are also important meaning carriers. We interpret as "speech" the movement and gestures of the body. The posture, the twinkle or glint in the eye, the turn of the mouth, or whatever, provide vital clues to the meaning of what is being said. To say, "I love you," with my words but not with my eyes is to tell you that I may not love you. To tell you, "I love you," without touching your hand or arm may be to tell you that my love is not strong. To touch the hand or arm of a mate or friend, perhaps to touch cheeks, is to provide another avenue of communication, an avenue of intense beauty and meaning if the gestures are sincere. In many situations words may not be needed and might, if used, reduce the quality of the communication. There are many ways of saying a simple phrase. The meanings vary with the use of each combination of words, voice, and action.

Gesture. The face and body, the eyes, the feet, the hands tell a great deal in conversation or speech. The narrower the boundaries of a communication, the smaller and more refined are the physical responses. The larger the audience, the more abundant and gross the gestures. Here, of course, we are concerned with interpersonal communication between family members. The need to talk but also to act in certain ways as we talk are major issues in a family. A wife or husband does not usually like to be gesticulated at although each likes physical animation from the other. To use much gross action in conversation may be a sign of a lack of confidence in wife or husband. But some cultural groups utilize energetic gestures even in casual conversations; notice Jewish and Italian persons in discourse. The culture of the persons has much to do with appropriateness of gesture. Northern Europeans use less overt action than southern Europeans. This bit of information was helpful to a wife of Swedish descent married to a man of Italian background.

Touch, as an issue in communication, is important—more important than can be accented here. The touch of hands and bodies, of lips and arms, are important to husband/wife, parent/child communication. In American and Canadian cultures children are often taught by precept or example that touching one another may lead to harmful intimacy. These children grow into adults and become cold, perhaps become unnaturally frigid, because they have been denied the warmth of legitimate physical contact. Probably every counselor has heard the soft but poignant plaintive, "I never remember a time when my father hugged me," or "Not only did my father never tell me he loved me, he never touched me in love." Even mothers have been accused of this omission by their adult children.

A man or woman having been reared without physical contact may expect significant discord in marriage. The human being cries out for intimacy. If he has been conditioned against intimacy, there will be disappointment and human loss. Some can give but not receive loving gestures, some receive but not give, some neither give nor receive. Happy marriages are open and free. Generally, they are tactile and understanding of human hunger for fulfillment. They both give and receive. Only a portion of this exchange is sexual, and that sexual exchange may be kept within appropriate boundaries. Both American and Canadian Christian communities need to review the restrictions they have put upon physical contact. There is loving physical touch that has no wrongful sensual connotation. It may be that the appropriate expression of intimacy in a young family might protect growing children from wrong expression later. Each human need may be legitimately met.

Signals. The wedding ring one wears, the clothes, the acceptable conduct, signal information to observers. Sloppy eating and poor grooming also communicate something. A woman who had lived with her husband for many years confided that she felt he was largely self-centered because of the manner in which he ate his food, the way he dressed, and the subjects of his interest. In these ways he broadcasted signals of his inner thought, or lack of it. It is likely that she had an accurate interpretation of his inner attitudes. But there is more. When the signals of one mate differ from those of the other, there will likely grow up feelings which will threaten happiness. Many refined women have lived unhappy lives because their husbands were crude in dress and manners, possessing a cultural style which, though appropriate to their rearing, was foreign to their wives.

Object. Appointments in one's home provide some information about a person so a caller will decide, even before meeting him, what he must be like and whether or not the caller wishes to believe what he has to say when he gets around to saying anything. The manner in which a house is furnished and maintained communicates something about and to husband, wife, and child. The messages are vital, for they speak of respect for one another— worth, care, beliefs, and the like. Mates should give attention to their home appointments to create the appropriate atmosphere which assists in understanding one another.

MARITAL PROBLEMS AND COMMUNICATION ENVIRONMENT

Marital problems may be related to environmental communications. Most persons little realize that where something is said, the time of day, and the distance one stands or sits from the person talked to may exert a crucial effect on the outcome of the communication. Considerable psychological aggression takes place through manipulation of these factors.

The place in which a communication takes place significantly influences the communication. Each person has his own "turf," the place where he has at least the authority advantage in any confrontation. This provides him a "one-up" situation. But in marital situations the best place to talk is wherever both husband and wife are the most comfortable.

A beautiful room, an ordinary room, an ugly room may actually change the meaning of what is said or done. We know that learning takes place more readily in beautiful surroundings, and persons are willing to dedicate themselves for longer periods of time to the tasks before them. There is reason to believe that some persons are so offended by their environmental circumstances that they never gain a sense of well-being in their marriages. Considerable research has been made on what happens to marriages which are negatively influenced by ugly apartments and slums. Persons unacquainted with the influences of poverty and ugliness may be ill-prepared to make judgments about men, women, and children who are conditioned by those factors.

The time at which a communication takes place relates to the effectiveness of that message. La Haye warns about the use of late hours for the introduction of a difficult subject. He states that 10:00–10:30 P.M. is questionable because the topic may affect the relationship and rest which the couple ought to have.[6] Early in the day is a problem if one member is a chronically late riser. After dinner (often a good time) may be limited because of the presence of small children. There is a best time for each couple, and attention should be given to its discovery. For most the best time should be when no appointment or interruption is expected and some time may be reserved before final decisions are made.

The distance or space between persons affects the message communicated. Each person holds a comfortable distance at which he will communicate most readily with others. We know this is commonly a greater distance with Caucasians than most other racial groups. This may contribute to some alienation from one another. Mates who maintain a cool distance between each other are generally less happy and feel that they are less loved than close demonstrative couples.

The development of effective listening habits is the beginning of excellence in communication. Persons may listen for social, educational, therapeutic, or analytical reasons. Social listening is to register and respond appropriately to ordinary greetings or general observations; educational is to develop the memory of facts or concepts for future recollection; therapeutic is to listen for the purpose of healing a troubled person; and critical listening is related to evaluative techniques and problem solving. To choose the wrong reason for listening may cause failure in this vital area of effective communications. Without a willingness to listen intently to one another, members of any family will tend not to communicate very well with each other.

Basic understanding of communications includes what is said, how it is said, and in what circumstances or environment. Happy families tend to work at improving both verbal and nonverbal communications.

NOTES

1. Thomas A. Harris, *I'm OK—You're OK* (New York: Harper & Row, 1967).

2. Brent Peterson, Gerald Goldhaber, Wayne Pace, *Communications Probes* (Palo Alto, Cal.: Science Research Associates [IBM], 1974).

3. Sven Wahlroos, *Family Communication* (New York: Macmillan, 1974).

4. Dwight Hervey Small, *After You've Said I Do* (Westwood, N.J.: Fleming H. Revell, 1968). Note chapters "Buttoned Lips and Boxed-in Lives" and "Circuit-Jammers."

5. Peterson, et al., *Communications Probes.*

6. J. Allan Petersen, ed., *The Marriage Affair* (Wheaton, Ill.: Tyndale House Publishers, 1971).

6

Divorce and Remarriage: A Fresh Biblical Perspective

DWIGHT H. SMALL

Divorce and remarriage is an increasingly visible reality in evangelical communities. Reexamination of the Scriptures suggests that we need a more open view than we have had in the past. However, this does not at all imply that the Bible treats divorce and remarriage as a Christian option. The divine intent for indissoluble marriage stands uncompromised. What compels a new pastoral approach is the question: What do we say to Christians who have decisively failed in marriage, whether for reasons within their control, or reasons relatively outside their control? What do we say to them when the only appropriate life option seems to be that of restoring a home and family life for themselves and their children through remarriage—especially when the remarriage affords the first possibility of a truly God-honoring Christian union? Life has the promise of becoming complete again. Even one's place in the Christian community may once again be normalized. What do we say to these brothers and sisters in Christ?

Conventionally, evangelicals take one of three positions on di-

DWIGHT H. SMALL is associate professor of sociology at Westmont College, Santa Barbara, California. Previously he served a number of Presbyterian churches as minister. Mr. Small is a member of the counseling center at Westmont and has conducted marriage workshops in churches across the nation. His books include *Design for Christian Marriage; Christian, Celebrate Your Sexuality;* and *The Right to Remarry.* Mr. Small is married and has two daughters and three grandsons.

vorce and remarriage. First, Scripture allows no divorce and remarriage at all, citing Jesus' words in Mark 10 and Luke 16.
Second, divorce is allowable only on the ground of a partner's
sexual unfaithfulness, citing Jesus' words in Matthew 5 and 19,
with some allowing remarriage, others not. Third, divorce is per-
missible when an unbelieving spouse wants it, citing Paul's word
in 1 Corinthians 7, again with some granting remarriage, some not.
My presentation will offer a fourth option based on a less conventional but fully supportable biblical exegesis within a systematized
approach through theological ethics. This larger framework of
theological ethics becomes determinative.

Not every ethical declaration in Scripture can be universalized to
apply to all periods of redemptive history. Each biblical passage
has its own special context. Any position we take for ourselves
must fit within the particular ethic meant to govern the present
church age, not necessarily the past Mosaic period, or the future
established kingdom. In this fallen world, the will of God is ad-
ministered conditionally. Its unconditional application to mankind
was of necessity altered after the Fall. The Mosaic Law, regulatory
of the Old Testament period of redemptive history, was temporary.
Jesus' announcement of the kingdom ethic will have its complete
fulfillment only after the king returns and consummates his kingdom. Prior to that time, that ethic applies provisionally in the
church age. The church age anticipates the kingdom, but less than
full kingdom conditions prevail. It is a partial, preform of the kingdom at most, marked by failures among the redeemed, by God's
gracious forgiveness, and by restoration to life's higher possibilities
for relationships as God intended.

God's original intent, expressed in Genesis 2:24, envisions marriage as an enduring, indissoluble union of two persons in their
totality—mind, spirit, and body. It is a life partnership—more than
a formal contract, more than an exclusive sexual union, more than
living together domestically as a couple. Its essence comprises
mutual love and full personal commitment. Anything less is not
true marriage.

In Mosaic Law, the Old Testament provision for divorce and
remarriage manifested the operation of God's conditional will, the
expression of his transcendent grace. Likewise, the New Testament

Epistles provide forgiveness and the divine response of renewing grace for every sin and failure in the believer's life.

Beginning with the Pentateuch, we find neither a marriage nor a divorce law. We look in vain for any law prohibiting divorce and remarriage. Now, were there to be absolute divine prohibition, it surely would have been set forth unambiguously in Mosaic Law with its severe sanctions. It is not. Instead, there is regulatory law, forbidding divorce under certain conditions, making it mandatory under others (see Deut. 23, Ezra 10, and related passages). Only in special circumstances—for example, Malachi 2—are there allusions to divine disapproval. Never in the Old Testament is remarriage in question, nor are there sanctions of a legal, social, or ecclesiastical nature anywhere imposed upon divorced, remarried persons.

Deuteronomy 24:1–4 takes divorce and remarriage for granted— something that has been true of the entire history of the Jewish people. Disapproval is nowhere expressed, but instead legal recognition and regulation is the theme. In this passage the reason for divorce is left extraordinarily ambiguous—I think with divine deliberation—bringing about the age-long controversy between the rabbinic schools of Hillel and Shammai a century before Jesus, then later on the Pharisees' questioning of Jesus, and even today the differing renderings of Deuteronomy 24:1–4 in modern Bible versions. Jewish opinion then and now favors the more liberal grounds of Hillel—divorce for many causes—not the single ground of adultery advocated by Shammai. For adultery, the Old Testament penalty invariably was death. Other sins of sexual uncleanness carried specific penalties, but never divorce. God granted divorce as a gracious concession, his original intent having become subject to his conditional will for sinful mankind.

JESUS ON DIVORCE

Concerning divorce in the New Testament, there are four separate statements of Jesus, all recorded in the synoptic Gospels, plus one major passage in 1 Corinthians 7. Matthew presents a very special Gospel context because Jesus' use of the exceptive clause— "except for unchastity"—appears only there, in chapters 5 and 19. In Matthew 19:3–12, the most complete passage of the four, Jesus is not addressing his church but is answering the Pharisees' questions relating to Mosaic Law. These interpreters and guardians of the Law sought to trip up Jesus by compelling him to take sides in the Hillel-Shammai controversy. Here Jesus speaks to Israel under the Law. It is questionable whether we can generalize from this context so as to apply his words to those outside Mosaic Law. But whatever the context, Jesus did point to God's original purpose of indissoluble marriage and confirmed the continuation of that purpose. Clearly, man is not intended to alter what God established. Whether sinful conditions do in fact alter what God has established is another question. There is a world of difference between allowing divorce and remarriage as an extreme solution to inescapable failure, and treating divorce and remarriage on the other hand as though they were acceptable options. Notice, too, that Jesus said, "It was not so from the beginning," that is, before the Fall. But this is not the same as suggesting that pre-Fall conditions were completely restorable from then on, even in his church. In other words, Jesus did not deny the place of divorce in the fallen world. He simply pointed to the creative ideal.

According to Jesus, adultery is the only exception. This is tantamount to saying that sexual exclusivity is intrinsic to the marriage bond, not that it is the whole of that bond, but intrinsic to it. When violated, an intrinsic break occurs in that bond that is of fundamental significance. Divorce may then follow permissibly.

Why did Jesus not include this exception in the declarations reported by Mark and Luke? Conventional explanations are quite unconvincing. It cannot be that Jesus stated two contradictory principles on separate occasions; nor can we accept these contradictions as inaccurate reporting. Much less can we tolerate the idea that Matthew put words in Jesus' mouth to make him conform to the Old Testament. And what can we say to the theories that Jesus made an exception because he was thinking of the premarriage state of Jewish betrothal (illustrated by Joseph's thought to divorce Mary privately because she was pregnant at the time of their betrothal), or that Jesus was thinking of consanguineous marriage— marriage between blood relatives involving prohibited degrees? These theories are implausible since Scripture nowhere indicates this meaning, and one would expect a sure explanation were this the case. The natural view is that of regular marriage, reinforced by the fact that the Pharisees were testing Jesus concerning the Deuteronomy controversy which related to regular marriage. There was no controversy whatever about either betrothal aberrations or consanguineous marriage. I propose the following explanation which involves no fanciful altering of the contexts and no inherent contradictions.

May it not be that on the two occasions reported by Mark and Luke where no exceptive clause is included, Jesus affirmed the original divine principle, unequivocally aligning himself with the creative intent? Then, may it not be in the two occasions reported by Matthew, where the exceptive clause is included, that Jesus was facing the realities of the fallen world, disclosing the one exception which intrinsically destroys the marital bond and alters the basic principle? It is not at all uncommon in life as we know it to state a principle in its pure intent, elsewhere restating that same principle in terms of allowable exceptions in view of extenuating circumstances not originally envisioned. The condition of human sinfulness and failure calls for such restatement. This interpretation frees us to accept both forms of Jesus' statement— without the exceptive clause, or with it.

Jesus said that persons who divorce and remarry commit adultery. Quite likely he is not speaking of literal adultery but of the technical consequence of these persons' failure to fulfill God's purpose. Intrinsically, one bond has been broken and another substituted in its place. Over against the perfect will of God this is a form of adultery. This is not the same as a continuing state of adultery. It is an act, and an act subject to God's forgiving grace. Remember, Jesus also equated the lustful look with adultery; it, too, is subject, not to legal sanction, but to forgiveness. To remarry is to acknowledge adultery insofar as it is not God's perfect plan, but the step is taken with the sense that God's grace permits it, and within his conditional will he can bless it. God does not deal with us practically on the basis of our performing perfect righteousness, but on the basis of two realities: our limited ability to appropriate the perfect resources in Christ, and his unfailing grace.

Jesus did not say that remarriage is forbidden because of the label perfect righteousness must put upon it, nor that it cannot in any sense have the blessing of God. What he seems to imply is that it involves: (1) a disruption that is technically sinful, (2) an impediment that cannot simply be dismissed, and (3) acknowledgment with penitence before God can bless a new marriage. Of course, the degree of personal responsibility for marital dissolution varies with the individual, with not a few relatively innocent of the causes which brought about their marital dissolution. Will not God in his grace do a new thing for them?

PAUL ON DIVORCE

Curiously, in the Epistles the only major subject reference is 1 Corinthians 7. Here Paul says he's answering specific inquiries of the Corinthians. We must be careful not to limit New Testament thought to those particular questions, asked by that particular church, at that particular time, under those particular circumstances. For Paul declares in verse 26 his grave concern for what he terms the present, or impending, distress. This concern governs his whole discussion in chapter 7. It very well may have affected his counsel about remarriage especially. If so, the application to our times is greatly circumscribed and conditioned. This is certainly true of Paul's strong advocacy of singlehood in that chapter.

Incidentally, neither Peter, James, nor John touch on the subject; nowhere in the Epistles is the word of Jesus directly quoted; and there is no systematic teaching anywhere, only Paul's response to these specific inquiries. Even with that opportunity before him, Paul doesn't go into any critical situations as we today would judge them or into their possible redemptive solutions. So it simply doesn't follow that he might not have had something else to say had they raised other questions concerning impossible marital situations. This relative absence of teaching in the Epistles scarcely lends encouragement to judgmental, disciplinary attitudes and actions. Rather, it seems it should encourage forgiveness, acceptance, and provision for restoration! What greater ethic might the church announce than this?

Interestingly, despite the extensive passages on church discipline, especially in the Corinthian letters, no church discipline is associated with divorced, remarried persons; yet adultery was to be disciplined in the church. Nor is divorce and remarriage ever mentioned in the listings of sins catalogued in the Epistles. Does this not provide a pastoral cue? What scriptural grounds have we, really, for discriminating against the remarried when it comes to service in the church? When Paul says that a pastor or elder is to be the husband of one wife (Titus 1:6; 1 Tim. 3:2), he probably refers to monogamy as opposed to the polygamy widely practiced in the heathen world. With this many ancient and modern authorities agree. Paul does not say "one who has been married only once," but clearly "the husband of one wife." Literally, a remarried man indeed fulfills this requirement.

In 1 Corinthians 7 Paul alludes to Jesus' word, but does not quote him. At critical points, in fact, his own word is notably different, both in what he adds and in what he omits. Paul is interestingly adaptive to the pastoral situation. Jesus has been limited to teaching those still under the Law; Paul was not. Jesus had been concerned with pure principles of righteousness; Paul, with specific problem situations and their redemptive solutions. Paul affirms that in general Christians are not to divorce, not that they could not, but should not (1 Cor. 7:10–11). He adopts, not a legal approach, but a pastoral one. He simply states the fundamental principle first; at this point no exceptional circumstances concern him. This is as it was with Jesus in Mark's and Luke's report of his basic principle. This is also the case in 1 Corinthians 7:39 and Romans 7:1–4. But this is not Paul's final consideration. He will go farther, even as Jesus did according to the report by Matthew of his exceptive clause.

Incidentally, the word *separate,* according to our best lexicons, clearly means divorce. Actually, neither Greeks nor Romans, and surely not Jews living in Hellenistic Corinth, would have understood separation which left marriage undissolved. There was no such thing as legal separation. Separations as such were regarded as morally scandalous in that society. So for Paul to have meant mere separation without complete dissolution would have required on his part a definite explanation.

Having stated the general principle "should not divorce," Paul adds concerning the wife, "but if she does"—a tacit, realistic acknowledgment that divorce inevitably will occur in this fallen world even among believers—then, "Let her remain single or be reconciled to her husband." Where reconciliation remains a viable hope, this counsel is unquestionably right. Let me inject a strong personal word that our pastoral responsibility is to pursue every possibility for reconciliation. This is our primary task. It is never the pastor's place to suggest divorce, regardless of how hopeless he may view the situation. Paul's alternative to the wife to remain single was at least good counsel for that time and place, in view of the present or impending distress to which he refers, and which led him earlier in the chapter to prefer the single state over marriage. Under more normal circumstances the single state would not have been considered preferable for any number of biblical and social reasons. What is notable is that Paul gave advice that Jesus did not give. Nor would Jesus have allowed divorce for the reason of adultery—as he did—only then to have commanded reconciliation. Circumstances certainly altered Paul's approach.

Now, it would seem that Paul might have settled the Corinthians' questions rather simply by just quoting Jesus' words exactly and letting them stand for all situations. That he did not do so raises the question of whether the Holy Spirit instructed Paul that Jesus' word was not meant to cover this situation. Apparently so, for Paul proceeds to give his own distinct counsel.

Next, he turns to the Corinthians' question about believers married to unbelievers (1 Cor. 7:12-16). Again, he goes beyond anything Jesus said or intimated, seeming even to contradict Jesus— that is, if we limit Jesus' thought to his recorded words. Paul begins typically, and rightly, with the basic principle which necessarily underlies all further considerations: Christians should not divorce pagan partners because they are pagan. But what if the pagan partner, who does not live according to Christian principles, wants out? Paul says he has no word from the Lord—which seems tantamount to saying that the word that he did have from the Lord doesn't meet this situation. So, under the Spirit's guidance, he ventures a judgment which is quite different from anything Jesus said.

If the unbelieving spouse wants a divorce, Paul says, "Let it be so" (v. 15). Notice, the word *separate* means divorce. Certainly, it is understandable that what the pagan spouse wanted was more than mere separation. That would have left his marital status in limbo and thwarted his desire for another partner. And incidentally, this has nothing to do with desertion, as is often claimed. What the pagan partner wanted was clear-cut divorce, freedom to follow his inclinations. Customarily, this is exactly what occurred.

So Paul says, "Let it be so." He argues that one is not to fight for formal retention of marriage at any cost, whether on the basis of the creative intent or the words of Jesus. He doesn't urge the Christian to try every means possible to save the marriage—the unvarying modern pastoral approach. Neither does he so much as hint that the Christian partner will be guilty of adultery if he or she remarries—a strange omission if he were following Jesus strictly! Nor does he counsel the Christian partner to remain single in hopes of an eventual reconciliation should the pagan spouse be converted and want to return.

Paul continues, "In such a case a brother or sister is not bound." Not bound to what? Our best lexicons say "not enslaved, not held by constraint of law or necessity." A legal term for over two hundred years in Greece, whether used with reference to releasing a slave or divorcing a spouse, the words *not bound* meant complete release from the bonds of the former contractual relationship. The bill of divorcement was called "a bond of relinquishment," which meant "no longer bound." In the New Testament, this word *to bind* —stronger of two possible words—expresses the total binding of one person to another; *not bound* means the exact opposite. One is no longer enslaved to such a marriage; the contractual bond is broken, relinquished as though it had never existed. This leaves no impediment whatever to remarriage, and none is mentioned by Paul.

Paul might have stopped here, but he didn't. He introduces a scale of relative values—something Jesus did not do—saying, "For God has called us to peace." His thought is that marriage is to be characterized by peace, not slavery to an empty contractual relationship. On God's scale of relative values for his people in the fallen world prior to the kingdom, indissoluble marriage stands high, for it alone conforms to his original intent. But personal peace is also high—higher in fact than any mere retention of a marriage which at heart is not a loving union of total persons, but a semblance only, a fraud. Such formal recognition only may in fact be destructive of all values at long last. Better such marriage be dissolved than that peace be rendered impossible. Persons are not to be sacrificed in order to preserve a bond no longer viable. Marriage was made for man, not man for marriage! In some cases, divorce and remarriage may rightfully be utilized in the service of the higher good—spiritual, emotional, personal peace without which no Christian can experience normal well-being. While all divorce is cause for sadness, not all divorces are destructive of personal and family values in this world. There are genuine instances in which divorce is a blessed release to new promise and life. We must not deny this reality in our zeal to protect all couples from the tragedy of divorce. So, then, sometimes a tragic moral choice must be made, determining the lesser of two evils. According to Jesus, the Old Testament divorce concession was because of their "hardness of heart." Paul grounds his concession on personal peace in the believer's life.

As if this were not sufficient to make his point, Paul adds, "Wife, how do you know whether you will save your husband? Husband, how do you know whether you will save your wife?" (v. 16). Marriage, comments William Barclay, is not a missionary institution! There's no guarantee that formal retention of an impossible marriage will eventually lead to the salvation of the recalcitrant partner. Don't count on that, says Paul.

A crucial question is whether this principle extends beyond the question of pagan spouses. What would Paul have said, for example, if an immature Christian husband wanted out, one who had been counseled over a long period of time, one who continually rendered peace impossible, such that the wife was breaking down emotionally, physically, and spiritually, and the children were fear-ridden and questioning the very worthwhileness of marriage itself? We cannot know, for Paul doesn't deal with any such situations. It is possible that God recorded this one situation to illustrate the place of pastoral discretion—counseling extreme situations in the context of what seems spiritually best for the individual.

WHAT IS THE APPLICATION FOR TODAY?

We have looked closely at the relevant passages of Scripture, but our task is not yet complete. We must now place the subject in a larger framework—theological ethics. What is the means by which God deals with his people ethically as a result of Calvary and the resurrection? The crucial question is our interpretation of the kingdom ethic which Jesus announced in such contexts as the Sermon on the Mount. Do we expect to fulfill perfectly that ethic in these times before the kingdom is established at his coming? If not, what is God's response to our failures? Does he apply his ethic as a law, imposing certain sanctions upon the failing?

All Jesus' declarations on divorce and remarriage are found in the synoptic Gospels, in his teaching concerning the kingdom to be established under his personal reign. In the Sermon on the Mount, sample kingdom laws are announced, typical of the fuller body of law that will govern the messianic kingdom. George Eldon Ladd convincingly demonstrates the dual nature of the kingdom, consummated in apocalyptic power at the end-time when Christ returns, yet genuinely though only partially present prior to that in the church age. With the first coming of Christ, the kingdom did indeed enter history in advance of its future consummation. At present it works secretly among men. Necessarily, there are limitations to its ethical fulfillment inasmuch as kingdom conditions are only partially present. Even individual Christians represent varying degrees of sanctification and personal maturity. Consequently, failures can and do occur at every level of Christian experience, including the marital. This requires an ethic adapted to this interim period of the church age, congruent with prekingdom conditions. Kingdom law is never to be compromised; nevertheless it must be provisionally adopted so as to leave room for God's forgiving, renewing grace in the event of failure. Thus the church age is marked by tension between kingdom demands in their radical perfection on one hand and the sins and failures of God's people on the other. But the consequence of failure—if the Epistles teach us anything at all—is not the severe sanction of inflexible law, but rather the ever-available forgiveness and restoration of grace.

Helmut Thielicke helps us with his description of the two aeons that make up redemptive history. Draw one circle to represent the Old Aeon, the fallen world. Draw another circle to represent the New Aeon, God's kingdom. The Old Aeon stretches from the Fall of man to the return of Christ. The kingdom is then established;

the New Aeon is here. Thus it appears that the New Aeon directly follows the Old, but no. The kingdom broke through in advance of its consummation at the first coming of Christ. Thus the church is a preform of the kingdom, a partial manifestation of it. The two aeons do not follow, one upon the other; they overlap. The church age is the overlapping period in redemptive history, an interim period which incorporates elements of both the Old Aeon and the New Aeon, yet is distinct from either.

Christian ethics, it now appears, concerns itself with the church's temporary ensconcement in the Old Aeon, in the fallen world. We are in that period, with the demands of the New Aeon upon us, yet living provisionally under the conditions of the fallen world, the Old Aeon. What bridges this dual set of conditions is the transcendent grace of God. In every Christian failure, where there is confession and penitence and new commitment to God's will, there is superabounding grace. Christians sometimes do have to make the tragic moral choice of the lesser of two evils on a relative scale of values, choosing whatever remains the best option open to them following failure to meet God's pure will. In such a field of tension, where perfect righteousness is not always possible, Christians must seek the Holy Spirit's power to fulfill God's demands, all the while living provisionally within the possibility of needing his forgiveness and renewal. This is redemptive reality!

Kingdom righteousness is presently attainable to a greater degree by some, to a lesser degree by others. Capacity to appropriate the resources in Christ will differ from individual to individual. Thus the kingdom has entered history without presently transforming it. But there, in the interim, is the healing, restoring ministry of God!

One divorce context is the Sermon on the Mount. Here we have kingdom ethics without any reference to redemptive grace in its process of forgiveness. The Sermon on the Mount is not concerned with the field of tension between God's demands and man's failures. The Sermon on the Mount cannot be applied to the church without being qualified in terms of God's gracious response to failure as announced in the Epistles.

In final consideration, as marital dissolution always displays human failure at best, sin at worst, may not a Christian remarriage display redemptive, renewing grace? May not God be glorified in a new marriage where mutual love and commitment and desire for his will enable a couple to fulfill a truly "one-flesh" enduring marriage?

So when a divorced Christian asks, "Have I the right to remarry?" I reply: The right to remarry is neither a personal nor a Christian right; it is not a right at all. It relates solely to God's grace and is not related to cause. The relatively innocent and the relatively guilty alike are denied a case for cause, removing all remarriage from the question of which is valid and which is not. All divorce is failure to meet God's standard and hence is sin; all parties alike need God's grace. But to all divorced Christians— guilty as well as innocent—renewing grace is available. The sole condition is confession, true penitance, and the desire to go on to fulfill God's will. This grace relates only to those who have truly tried and decisively failed. To them, and at the time of their final, irreversible decision, God comes with forgiveness and renewing grace.

7

Divorce and Remarriage: Practical Implications for the Church

LARS I. GRANBERG

"Pastor, I'm a second-class member of this church!" The speaker, a pleasant-looking man in his late thirties, was clearly upset.

"How so?" asked his pastor.

"I've been divorced! That's the unpardonable sin, it seems! The way things operate here it seems you can be greedy, a vicious backbiter, cheat on your income tax reports, peddle rabid racial prejudice, be a slum landlord, or guilty of just about every other sin in the book, and be in good standing. Not if you've been divorced, though. It's my nature to want to get involved, but here I feel frozen out. I'm not eligible. It's as though I had leprosy. I thought the Christian gospel meant a fresh start to the penitent."

The pastor who shared this conversation grimaced a bit, "It's true, you know. We do an especially poor job of ministering to single persons and to the divorced. How I wish some members of my congregation didn't feel obliged to keep rubbing in their disapproval of divorce by keeping divorced persons on the fringe.

LARS I. GRANBERG is dean of the Division of Social Sciences and professor of psychology at Hope College, Holland, Michigan. He was president of Northwestern College, Orange City, Iowa, for nine years, and before that taught at Hope and at Fuller Theological Seminary, where he was also dean of students. Dr. Granberg also conducts human development workshops for faculty, clergy, and students. He is the author of *Marriage is for Adults Only*. He and his wife Carol have three children and two grandchildren.

The worst of it is that I don't believe our congregation is at all untypical."

A generation ago such an attitude toward divorced persons was widespread in theologically conservative churches. Apparently it prevails sufficiently today to call for careful assessment.

UNDERSTANDING THE DIVORCED PERSON

Divorce is, to be sure, a serious matter. The biblical ideal for marriage is a covenanting together to lifelong faithfulness and devoted helpfulness between husband and wife. Regrettably, those who stay married fall short of this ideal as well as those who divorce. Divorce, however, cuts off further possibility for improving the relationship and inevitably results in a great deal of suffering, especially when children are involved. One may well echo the title of a recent article, "Too Many Divorces Too Soon."

But the church must do more than merely deplore. First, we as the church are faced with an undeniable reality: There is a growing number of divorced persons within the fellowship of the church. Too often the response to them is ambivalent. Church members are glad these persons seek the fellowship of the church. They've not, however, lived up to biblical ideals against divorce. One must not, then, be too enthusiastic about them, lest they think what they did is all right. And so the "freeze out." A divorce is an accomplished fact. It cannot be undone. Even remarriage to the same person, while it may restore the legal status, does not undo the distressing experience. To minister to divorced persons in the name of Jesus Christ, the church must begin by accepting the divorce as an accomplished fact. Grandstand quarterbacking, second guessing is useless. "Why didn't they . . . ?" or "Why couldn't they have . . . ?" may cover matters that divorced persons have to understand for their own personal healing and growth. Answers to such questions are best worked out by the divorced person in consultation with a pastor or counselor.

It is not the task of the church to enter into an endless circle of recrimination. Rather as messengers of the gospel—God's good news to sinners that there is in Christ forgiveness, renewal, and hope for those who seek it—we should be asking, not "Why didn't *they?*" but "Where do *we* go from here?" In seeking the fellowship of the church, divorced persons have a right to expect that they are associating themselves with a helping, healing community.

Our Lord dealt with people as he found them. He did not, for example, fulminate against the much-married Samaritan woman he met at Jacob's well. What he did instead was to identify himself to her as the long-awaited Messiah (John 4:25, 26). To the notorious woman of the streets who anointed his feet in the house of Simon the Pharisee he said, "Go in peace" (Luke 7:50). To Zacchaeus, the despised chief tax collector, Jesus said, "Come down; for I must stay at your house" (Luke 19:5). Dealing with people in this manner was not sanctifying the status quo. Rather, our Lord understood that to help people become what they can be one must love them as they are.

Why then, in view of our Lord's example, are Christians ambivalent toward divorced persons, even those within the fellowship of faith? The analysis which follows is necessarily speculative and tentative. It is based upon impressions gained from a lifelong association with church members and a good many years as a professional counselor and not upon a scientifically controlled survey. The suggestions set forth do represent, I believe, useful working hypotheses to deal with the problem of inappropriate attitudes within a congregation.

First, the presence of divorced persons arouses uneasiness in some persons over their own marriage. "Most men lead lives of quiet desperation," Henry Thoreau observed more than a century ago. This description, alas, applies with accuracy to the way some married couples, Christians included, live together. Many marriages, it seems, are held together by cellophane tape and baling wire. In every congregation one is likely to find couples living together and wondering how much more they can bear from each other or vaguely dissatisfied couples who feel there ought to be more to marriage than what they've managed to achieve. Divorced persons may well confront these couples rather acutely with the condition of their own marriages which are endured rather hopelessly or kept going out of propriety or duty. To these people the presence of divorced persons is a constant reminder that there is another way. ("Maybe it would be better to call it off!") This uneasiness could, of course, lead to constructive steps to improve the marriage, but many people prefer a deadly inertia to the pain of new beginnings. And because their marriage is shaky, they reason: Since those divorced people didn't hesitate to break up their own marriage, they'd probably not hesitate to break up ours if one of us happens to suit their fancy!

Second, some people are preoccupied with the aura of sexual misbehavior that often accompanies divorce. Sexual infidelity is a factor in divorce actions. Its frequency may be exaggerated in the public mind as a result of highly publicized instances involving people in the political, sports, or entertainment worlds. The Christian's reaction to this can be rather complex. One gets the feeling from some very proper Christians that these divorced people really shouldn't have all that fun and still be forgiven. Like the psalmist (Ps. 73) they seem to be asking, "Of what advantage is it for me to be faithful to my spouse when the wicked, who are unfaithful, have advantages and equal standing in the church?"

Then arises the problem Sigmund Freud made so central in his explanation of human behavior: unacknowledged sexual impulses or desires. People are most likely to react with the particular ambivalence described above when they have failed to acknowledge and to deal constructively with the sexual aspects of their nature. Usually such persons try to cope with their sexuality by keeping it out of their awareness. Many persons or situations are troublesome when one's repressed sexuality is not understood for what it is, for in such situations a person becomes subject to vague but intense feelings of threat. Given, then, the popular association of divorce and sexual misbehavior, anyone seeking to avoid his or her own sexuality through repression may well find the presence of divorced persons a source of discomfort.

To be whole one must acknowledge and deal with all elements of his or her nature, learning to bring them to captivity in Christ. The Bible sets forth a wholesome, constructive theology of sex that needs to be taught systematically and regularly by the church.

Those threatened by divorced persons because they cannot cope with their own sexuality remind us that the church must do a far better job of countering both the casual, hedonistic approach to sex so vociferously propogated today and the opposite tendency to regard the denial of sexuality as "spiritual." The Bible teaches a view of human nature that places value on both body and spirit, especially when in proper relationship.

Third, certain church members feel called upon to exact the pound of flesh, that is, make sure these sinners (divorced persons) are sufficiently penitent. However, can one tell? One way to ensure penitence, some think, is to treat offenders like pariahs. In the English public (that is, private) schools, for example, there was (or is) a custom of dealing with offenders by "sending them to Coventry." Offenders were to be ignored, treated as though they weren't there. Fellow students didn't talk to them or include them in games or parties. Except for passing food without comment at meals, it was as though they had ceased to exist. This game of "freeze out" to punish offenders is quite different from the Apostle Paul's instruction to the Christians at Corinth. He did, to be sure, direct them to excommunicate an impenitent participant in incest (1 Cor. 5:2), but in his second letter Paul instructs those same Christians that having made their point they should quickly take initiative and "turn to forgive and comfort him, or he may be overwhelmed by excessive sorrow. So I beg you to reaffirm your love for him" (2 Cor. 2:7, 8).

It is not our place as Christians to demand for some interminable period a hangdog, skulking, "pardon me for living" attitude from those we regard as offenders, in order to test their penitence. Jesus Christ clearly forbids his people to sit in judgment. He instructed us to tell the story of redemption in Christ, forgiveness for sin, hope for the future—all in the context of a fellowship of love, encouragement, and mutual burden-bearing.

After all, a good many divorced persons have been very deeply wronged. Given a choice many of them would have preferred not to be divorced. Or they felt driven to it by a desperation beyond the comprehension of those of us not in a similar situation. In this connection one is reminded of Winston Churchill's response to those Englishmen who wanted harshest measures taken against citizens of occupied countries who collaborated with the occupying Nazi forces. Churchill said, "Let no man who has not endured what they endured venture to pronounce judgment upon them." Such wise words reflect the spirit of our Lord. Of course the church does not promote divorce. In principle it would prefer that divorce did not occur. But that is not justification for its members to reduce divorced persons to second-class status. The church also takes a position against rudeness, cruelty, cheating, injustice, and exploitation of the poor and helpless. Yet these same church members do not ascribe second-class status to those who are rude or cruel or unjust. Human perfection is, after all, a fruit of grace not law. True penitence and the fruit of the Spirit cannot be coerced.

THE PERSONAL COST OF DIVORCE

Let us expurge from our minds the vision of "the gay divorcée." Divorce is seldom, if ever, the casual, gleeful legalized mate-swapping some people envision it. Few people are so unfeeling about a relationship rooted in love and entered into with high hopes. A more realistic idea of the personal cost of divorce is suggested by the titles of two articles which recently appeared in *Redbook*: "The Myth of the Civilized Divorce" and "It's Never a Nice Divorce."

Joseph Epstein probably spoke for most divorcées when he described his own experience as

> . . . an emotional ravaging that, short of starvation, imprisonment, disease and death itself, is probably equal to most that the world has to offer. . . . to go through a divorce is still . . . to go through a very private hell.[1]

> . . . to divorce is to own up to one's own dismal failure. . . . whatever else a divorce might be . . . it is an enormous personal failure.[2]

There is little here of "the gay divorcé." Whatever reality there may be in this image is, I believe, another version of Pagliacci the clown, who laughs while his heart breaks. Who of us, after all, would parade his hurt before an indifferent world?

Divorce, then, is a source of anguish. Waves of fear, loneliness, confusion, guilt, and anxiety for the future wash over a person as his marriage disintegrates. Even when the divorce is uncontested, the adversary nature of the legal process by which a divorce is effected seldom fails to add large doses of bitterness and resentment toward one's former mate. Epstein continues:

> . . . divorce has the greatest number of ways for the combatants to injure each other. . . . people who are merely imperfect are turned into all-too-perfect predators, each ready to savage the other.[3]

Battles over alimony, property division, custody of children, and visitation rights erode the best intentions to be decent and to make concessions. The raw emotional wounds generated as a by-product of the legal process endure. Bitterness may continue to fester near the surface for many years. Some never work their way through it. It is usual to feel betrayed and cheated. Our newspapers frequently remind us of this in the number of assaults, rapes, and murders perpetrated on former spouses, their parents, or new mates by divorced mates. Suicide among divorced men and women is three to four times higher than among married men and women.

Shattering as the process of divorcing or being divorced may be, this is only the beginning. "What now?" Divorce uproots. A life pattern has been destroyed and with it many of the bench marks by which a person orients himself. To be married is to define oneself in relation to one's mate and one's marriage. One's social life has been structured by the marriage. Now adrift and very lonely, how will one ever get through the long evenings? How should one think about himself? Must one be relegated pretty much to the company of other divorced persons? Those with whom one formerly socialized seem awkward and uneasy in one's presence. Sadness over the destruction of what was once so good catches up the person in unguarded moments. To listen to a group of divorced persons trying to help one another put their lives back together is to hear unmistakably their deep sense of failure and their bewilderment. Small wonder that those divorced persons who have neither the support and understanding of their family nor of a Christian community that cares and reaches out to them seek refuge in alcohol and casual sex.

And then there are the children. This is the hardest part. A gnawing sense of guilt troubles both the parent granted custody and the one not granted custody. The one with custody wonders how he can ever be an adequate parent alone. Involvements with one's children take on such a crucial quality. Every situation or decision becomes a test. There is a dreadful need to prove oneself adequate as a parent. So one seeks advice. This can be shattering, for one runs smack into what someone described as "the contradictory cacophony of 'experts.'" The amount of advice on how to rear children is formidable. Too much of it makes positive pronouncements when it would be wise to be tentative. The worst thing about this advice is that it tends to undercut a person's confidence in his or her own judgment as to what is and isn't good for children. Parenting, moreover, gets tiring and overwhelming when there's only one to do it. Occasional relief from parental responsibility would be so welcome, a sentiment well understood by almost any parent, but the single parent feels guilty and ashamed of such perfectly normal feelings.

Difficult as it is to be a single parent, Joseph Epstein, who received custody of his sons, speaks of the visitation rights granted the other parent as "in some respects . . . the keenest torture that divorce has to offer."[4] To oblige a mother or father to maintain and develop a parental relationship during a stated few hours each week is unreal. Normal parent-child relations aren't at all like that. Much of the time in ordinary family life parents and children just go on about their business. Sometimes they are directly involved with one another, but more often not. A word, a pat, a few sentences exchanged, a question answered, a decision handed down and, perhaps, discussed—these make up much of the business of parenting. Occasionally there's an extended conversation or a day-long outing. It is not at all a matter of being a full-time parent for one day or a few hours a week. Not only is such an arrangement unnatural, it is extraordinarily difficult for the parent who hasn't custody but who would like to share fully in important decisions that affect the children. It's really not possible on a part-time basis.

MINISTERING TO THE DIVORCED AND REMARRIED

The church's ministry consists in what the church is as well as what it does. While the church is the proclaimer of the good news that there is redemption and new life in Christ, it is also a fellowship of redeemed sinners. Too often the fellowship degenerates into an association of nice, proper, and self-righteous people. The early church's effectiveness in "turning the world upside down" lay in large measure in its example of a caring in community. The apostles held out, not only forgiveness and the hope of eternal life to a suffering world, but also membership in a community of concern and compassion. If the church is to be "salt" and "light" to the world today, then its congregations must examine carefully its teachings and, especially, the quality of its life together. "Take heed to yourself," Paul wrote to Timothy, "and to your teaching" (1 Tim. 4:16).

Suffering often serves as the crucible in which a person seeks a new direction for life. Whatever else it may be, divorce is a time of intense suffering. It can also be a time of opportunity. If, however, the experience of divorce is to be an occasion for personal healing, then suffering people need to find their place in a compassionate fellowship, a community which seeks diligently to maintain a climate in which it is safe to explore one's failures, desires, fears, and hopes. If a Christian congregation is serious about ministry, it must give heed to its climate of personal relations. What is needed for healing and growth is not a bland, superficial "niceness" but welcome, openness, warmth, freedom to struggle, and freely extended forgiveness.

As the church of Jesus Christ, our first task is to help divorced persons make a good transition to single life. They will need help as they cope with a new kind of loneliness for, having failed in their marriage, many divorced persons experience greater anxiety than before in all their relationships. Well-organized and well-led singles groups help provide a way to cope with loneliness, but they are not enough. Wider social opportunities should be available as the person feels ready for them. Christians are admonished to "practice hospitality" (Rom. 12:13) and not to "neglect to show hospitality to strangers" (Heb. 13:2). Christian homes are to share freely their warmth, love, personal interest, and concern with those beyond the family circle. Nor are the benefits gained from hospitality to divorced a one-way street. Married couples can learn much which can strengthen their own marriage from the experience of those whose marriage has failed.

Those given custody of children will need help with the children. The parent will need occasional relief from twenty-four-hour duty if perspective and enthusiasm for the task are to be maintained. Children of divorced homes need to experience a Christian family living together, opportunities to observe how husband and wife and parents and children relate to one another, to provide them with additional adult models. The lack of good adult models of both sexes is a disadvantage for children. Children and parent alike need the extended family support the community of believers could well supply.

Problems also arise in the ordinary course of existence. Household budgets, for example, can be bewildering if one has never worked with them. So can matters of insurance, taxes, automobile maintenance, and household repairs. And these are the easier ones. Yet there are persons in every congregation who could offer the practical help needed if some made it their business to attend to the needs of the widowed and the divorced. This task would require some organization, and someone would have to assume responsibility, but the task would not be overwhelming. The church can also see to it that counsel in the areas of emotional and social problems also is made available. Membership in the body of Christ means that the entire fellowship is involved in helping everyone to develop better family life, for "if one member suffers, all suffer together; if one member is honored, all rejoice together" (1 Cor. 12:26).

REMARRIAGE

What of remarriage? This is often a pressing concern and often premature. Good counsel from someone who has demonstrated he cares is particularly essential here. The policy on remarriage set forth by the Reformed Church in America is similar to the position taken by a number of Protestant denominations and one I commend for your consideration. It reads:

> A pastor may with good conscience officiate in the remarriage of divorced persons if in his judgment, and the judgment of the congregation's Board of Elders, the persons have met the following requirements: Recognition of personal responsibility for the failure of the former marriage, penitence and an effort to overcome limitations and failures, forgiveness of the former partner, fulfillment of obligations involved in the former marriage, and a willingness to make the new marriage a Christian one by dependence upon Christ and participation in His Church.[5]

Proceeding on the premise that the second marriage should be given a greater chance for success than the first, this policy wisely calls upon the divorced person who wishes to remarry to reflect carefully and penitently upon the ways he may have contributed to the breakup of the previous marriage. Unless this is done the person is likely to bring a destructive legacy to the new marriage. To be emotionally free of the earlier marriage one must seek a deep sense of God's forgiveness for one's failures and pray for grace to fully and freely forgive the former mate his or her offenses. He or she must also fulfill conscientiously any ongoing obligation to the former marriage.

Before remarriage the divorced person should have reached a new understanding of what Christian marriage involves together with a determination that this new marriage will be Christian in the fullest sense one can achieve. He or she and the prospective mate must be aware that they cannot accomplish this alone. A strong Christian marriage requires the help of God and the community of believers. The congregation available to the couple should encourage one another and share one another's burdens so that as the couple seeks a deeper relationship with Christ they can also grow in understanding and love for each other.

Example and a helping fellowship are necessary, but they are not enough. The church must also instruct continuously concerning biblical teaching in marriage and family life. A Christian understanding of marriage begins with clear teaching of God's intention for human life. The early church arose in the Hellenistic age, an era as relativistic, alienated, and adrift as our own. "The greatness of the early church consisted not only in the commitment of believers to one another but also in its presenting to the world an uncompromising model rather than an ethic of accommodation."[6]

Today's rampant individualism, which glorifies self-assertion and defines self-fulfillment as freedom to indulge oneself whimsically, must be shown by the church to be the perversion it is. The Bible teaches that marriage is a covenant within the larger covenant community. Marriage is never "nobody's business but my own." Members of the body of Christ are to be concerned for and accountable to one another. The church in turn has a right to expect her members to offer one another acceptance and forgiveness and to be faithful to their marriage covenant. Today's young people need such clear teaching on Christian marriage to provide an alternative to the secular world's ideas concerning sex and marriage which they absorb almost by osmosis.

Marriage is a gift of God, a treasure, which we have "in earthen vessels" (2 Cor. 4:7). As the fellowship of faith commanded by our Lord to love another (John 15:17), we must give higher priority to finding timely and comprehensive ways to help prevent marital failure, to help persons recover from marital failure, and to do a far better job of preparing the next generation for strong, joyous marriages rooted in Christ.

NOTES

1. Joseph Epstein, *Divorced in America* (New York: E. P. Dutton, 1975), p. 19.
2. Ibid., pp. 91–92.
3. Ibid., pp. 132, 134.
4. Ibid., p. 289.
5. Proceedings of the General Synod, Reformed Church in America, "Biblical Perspectives on Marriage, Divorce, and Remarriage," 1975, p. 170.
6. Ibid., p. 167.

8

Rapid Treatment
for a Troubled Marriage

ANDRE BUSTANOBY

The treatment of troubled marriages is not a complex, mystical procedure. Aside from specialized problems such as sexual dysfunction or difficulties arising from the rest of the family system, most dilemmas that couples face may be approached with the same therapeutic methodology.

I should say parenthetically, however, that no one should get the idea that counseling is a bag of tricks. It is a therapeutic relationship. If you have not read Charles B. Truax and Robert R. Carkhuff's book *Toward Effective Counseling and Psychotherapy: Training and Practice*,[1] do so. They point out that there are many approaches to counseling, but three characteristics are common to every successful counselor: accurate empathy, nonpossessive warmth, and genuineness. For the Christian counselor and pastor an integration of biblical truth in this therapeutic triad is also important.

I will describe a methodology that I have found very workable in bringing about rapid change in a troubled marriage. By rapid change I mean enabling a couple to function on their own after

ANDRE BUSTANOBY is a marriage and family counselor in Bowie, Maryland, and a member of the American Association of Marriage and Family Counselors. He is an ordained Baptist Minister and has pastored churches in Arlington, Virginia, and in southern California. He also conducts communication workshops and family life conferences. Mr. Bustanoby and his wife Fay have four sons.

eight to ten counseling sessions. If a couple is not making it on their own by then, one of them—or perhaps both—is resisting the process of change. The counselor's task becomes, then, not the marital problem but the resistance. In such a case further work on the resistance is needed.

I should say one further word before describing the procedure. I am assuming that the couple is *committed* to making the marriage work and that each is willing to *accept responsibility* for making it work. I will not work with a couple without this basic foundation. I do attempt to help them make such a commitment and accept responsibility, but we can go no further until this is done. With a cooperative, highly motivated couple the method I follow gets quick results. It involves four steps: (1) communication, (2) diagnosis, (3) negotiation for change, and (4) follow-up.

Communication. Almost without exception the couple with the troubled marriage is having a communication problem. If they knew how to talk to each other constructively, they would be solving their own problems. Their communication is probably following the pattern of attack, defense, and withdrawal.

I use two primary means of bridging the communication gap. The first is the Marital Communication Inventory.[2] This document is composed of 46 multiple-choice questions. The overall score for the average successful marriage is 105 out of a possible 138. A score below 95 indicates that communication is quite poor. In using this test, I tell the couple how each scored the communication in the marriage, and then I focus on the responses that reveal problem areas and have them talk about their communication style. Here we get down to specifics. For example, the first question is, Do you and your husband (or wife) discuss the manner in which the family income should be spent? If the answer is never, I want to know why. As I listen to the couple, I am able to pick up patterns in their communication style that keep them from conversing constructively. The pattern will often be an attack on the spouse and defense of self. By being very directive and not permitting attack or defense, I attempt to break up the couple's dysfunctional communication.

Sometimes a couple needs a more structured approach. The relationship may be so tense that they can't even talk in the counselor's office without fighting. I use a second device called the Revolving Discussion Sequence (RDS). This exercise slows down the process and keeps each from attacking the other. It is also designed to put each in touch with the other's feelings without judging whether or not those feelings are valid.

I start out by giving some basic rules. The couple must communicate in a way that does not sound attacking. This has to do with the content of what they say as well as the tone of the voice and body language (gesture, expression on the face, etc.).

Also, when they are spoken to, they must not defend themselves. When you try to tell a person how you feel and that person defends, explains, or justifies himself in any way, you will feel it's useless to tell him how you feel. The important thing is not to judge the rightness or wrongness of the feelings but to get in touch with what is there.

Finally, the emphasis must be on how each feels. This is conveyed with an "I" message rather than a "You" message. Instead of saying, "You are insensitive," it is better to say, "When my feelings are ignored, I feel like a nobody." Instead of saying, "You are a nag," say, "When I keep hearing what a poor husband I am, I feel beaten down, and I get angry."

The Revolving Discussion Sequence (RDS) attempts to teach these concepts by doing. I first ask one of the spouses to make a feeling statement to the other and to give the reasons for the feeling. The statement should be short and to the point. For example the wife may say to the husband, "I feel like a worthless person when you seem to have time and energy for everyone but me."

I then have the husband repeat the statement. This is to see if the husband heard exactly what she said and to slow down the exchange of words between them when tempers are hot.

She will then tell him if he correctly repeated what she said. If he doesn't, we repeat this step until it's right. He must be accurate.

The next step is for him to agree. He can agree with both the factuality of the statement and the feeling, or he may agree only that she feels that way. Many times the man will say something like, "But I don't give my time and energy to everyone but you." He wants to defend himself and argue the facts. I answer, "The facts are unimportant. The important thing is that your wife *feels* that way. Do you agree that she feels that way?"

The reasonable man will usually agree. Sometimes he will say, "No, she doesn't feel that way." My response is, "How do you know how she feels? Can you get inside her skin and feel her feelings? Are you saying that you don't want her to feel that way or that she has no right to feel that way? The fact of the matter is that she *does,* and only a change in your behavior will make her feel different."

Then I ask him to go through the same steps and make a feeling statement to her on the same theme. He may say, "I feel annoyed because you want more of my time than I'm willing to give you." She repeats the statement to check for hearing accuracy, and he corrects her where necessary. Then I tell her that she must agree with him. Sometimes a woman will say, "Well, shouldn't a husband be willing to give his wife his time before he gives it to total strangers?" My answer is, "The important thing is not to beat on him with shoulds and oughts but to listen to his feelings. When you understand his feelings, you're in a position to change what is causing problems in the relationship."

Couples spend a lot of time arguing about facts and shoulds and oughts, but they get nowhere. The primary thing in communication is to get in touch with feelings and the reason for them. You don't need to agree with the facts, but you must agree that the person feels as he says he does.

Sometimes couples have a hard time getting a feeling statement together; so I ask them to huddle with me. I help them put together a functional statement.

Sometimes one or both of the spouses will sabotage the process by *crazymaking,* a communication device we all use from time to time whenever the conversation begins to make us feel uncomfortable or trapped.[3] Crazymakers may derail you—get you off the subject—or they may overload with volume or content. The victim of crazymaking leaves the scene with his mind in confusion, actually feeling that he's going crazy. One couple went through a fifty-minute session of RDS and gave me just two functional statements. She was the crazymaker and spent the rest of the time derailing me, overloading me, and using every device she could to keep me from getting her to make a clear functional statement of her feelings.

Diagnosis—How to Identify What's Happening. My emphasis in diagnosis is interpersonal rather than intrapsychic. Intrapsychic has to do with behavior that is produced by internal condition of body and mind. Interpersonal has to do with behavior that is produced by our interaction with people. My diagnosis and therapy has to do largely with helping people understand their problem in terms of their relations with and reactions to other people.

Now I don't eliminate the intrapsychic entirely. Any client who tends to be depressive I refer to doctor for a complete checkup before he begins counseling. There could be a physical cause for his problem. A common problem I run into is menopausal syndrome. One of my clients has hypoglycemia, a physical disorder marked by an inability to maintain a proper blood sugar level. Deep depression and irrational anger mark this disorder.

Once I determine that the client is not suffering physical disorder, I diagnose and treat him with a view to interpersonal problems—how does he relate to significant other people in his life? If it is a family problem, I want to see how the entire family operates together. If it is a problem between husband and wife, I want to see them together and work with them together. It is extremely difficult to get anywhere with a marital problem by seeing just one spouse. You need the input that both offer.

The first step in diagnosis is to identify the fight issue. Psychologist George Bach suggests that there are eight basic problem areas in troubled marriages. He calls them "fair fight" issues—basic stimuli that cause the spouse to feel anger, threat, or any other negative emotion which in turn jeopardizes the relationship. The presenting issue may appear trivial, but the fact that it arouses heavy emotional involvement is a clue that it represents a more basic issue that threatens the well-being of either or both spouses.

For example, heated arguments often arise over tardiness, household disorganization, or the extravagance of one of the spouses. These are surface issues that hook into a more basic issue—the issue to which they ought to be giving attention. Perhaps tardiness really hooks into the basic issue of centricity—am I important?

When the husband is habitually indifferent about punctuality in dealing with his wife, she may feel, "I am unimportant to him. He seems to be on time for everyone but me." They may argue whether or not it's important to be on time for supper, with numerous side issues like the price of meat, but neither will win because each can assemble the facts to support his own view. Nevertheless, one thing cannot be argued: the wife *feels unimportant* and taken for granted by her husband. His protesting that she shouldn't feel that way is entirely out of order. The fact is that she *does* feel that way, and her husband's behavior causes the feeling. It is far easier for the husband to change his behavior than for the wife to change how she feels about that behavior. And, indeed, when he does change his behavior with respect to tardiness, he gives his wife the unmistakable message that he is listening to her, that he values her feelings, and that she is significant enough for him to change his ways.

Space does not permit my going into the fair fight issues in detail. My tapes on rapid treatment give fuller treatment as does my booklet, "How to Fight with Your Spouse." I will simply list the fight issues and identify what they are:

a. *Distance.* Every person has a psychological distance that is comfortable. Couples have problems establishing a proximity that is comfortable for both.

b. *Power struggle.* Who defines the relationship—one spouse or both? Do they struggle over who calls the shots?

c. *Trust.* Can feelings be exposed without fear of attack?

d. *Defense of self-identity.* Does each feel natural in his or her role as husband or wife?

e. *Sex.* Do they agree on what kind of sex, how often, when, and under what circumstances?

f. *Centricity.* Do both have the capacity to make the other feel important?

g. *Unrealistic illusions and expectations.* Do they expect things of each other that are unrealistic?

h. *Territorial aggression.* Every husband and wife has his or her own "turf." Is this turf violated by the other spouse?

Usually when a couple is taken through the Revolving Discussion Sequence and the Communication Inventory, the fight issue surfaces. When it does not become apparent through the use of these exercises, I employ yet another tool—the Caring Relationship Inventory.[4] The test measures five elements of love: affection, friendship, eros, empathy, and self-love. It also measures the concepts of being loved and deficiency love.

By comparing the test response to the real spouse and the ideal spouse, the counselor is able to find in what particular area love is being inhibited. In the average successful marriage the real and ideal spouses are found to have on an average only eleven differences. In a troubled marriage the differences can go as high as fifty. By discussing the differences the fair fight issue becomes clearer.

Negotiation for Change. Once I identify the fair fight issue or issues—there may be more than one—I'm ready for the change step. The first thing I want each spouse to do is to express feelings about the issue. At this point they will have become accustomed to the idea of expressing feelings through the use of RDS. Now I want them to express their feelings about the specific issue that is bothering them. For example, a woman's husband and children may be thoughtless about continually tracking mud into the house or not picking up their clothes or putting things away in the bathroom. The natural response of the wife is to attack them. She may tell them they're thoughtless. She may tell her husband that he must have been raised in a pigpen. This is bound to escalate into a free-for-all.

The fair fight issue is probably that of self-identity and centricity. What will her friends think of her when they see this messy house (self-identity)? What is more, she feels that when the family behaves like this they are taking her for granted; they're treating her like a slave (centricity).

When she identifies the issues, she must get in touch with her feelings about the issues. She can argue with her husband all she wants about the rightness of his picking up after himself, but he may argue that point, declaring that he doesn't have time or that he does pick up after himself or that's what he married her for. But when she gets in touch with her feelings and shares those feelings with her family, they can't argue with that. They may say that she shouldn't feel that way, but the fact is she *does,* and they are doing something to make her feel that way.

She may say, "When I see clothes lying around the house and dirty dishes stacked in the sink after I've cleaned up, I feel abused and put down. I feel responsible for keeping the house nice, but when this happens, I feel like a slave who is expected to go around picking up after the family." Centricity is the issue—"Am I important or am I a slave?" She may go on to say, "I can't leave the house a mess because I feel that the opinion my friends have of me is conditioned by how the house looks." Self-identity is also an issue—"What kind of a person will others think I am?"

A proper response to feelings like that is not, "You shouldn't feel that way." She does feel that way, and as a matter of fact, she has a right to feel that way because her basic human dignity is being destroyed—centricity and self-identity.

I must add that these feelings must be communicated without attack or defense. Attack and defense throw up barriers to good communication. When you verbally attack, you force your spouse to defend himself. He does so by rationalizing or justifying his behavior, and you invite counterattack from your spouse which is met by your own defense.

When you refuse to attack, you need not justify your feelings. Attack demands justification, but your feelings need no justification when there is no attack or accusation.

An example of both attacking and nonattacking communication may help. A husband is repeatedly late for supper. He seems indifferent about punctuality and permits any little thing to delay him. When he arrives late for the third time in so many days, his wife says in an accusatory tone and with agitated gestures, "You're late again. Look at this supper. It's cold. I went to a lot of hard work, and you spoiled it all."

She has attacked her husband! His response will be to justify his lateness and to attack her for not being understanding or placing too much importance on supper.

Let's see how this might be handled in a nonattacking way. First, she should make sure the timing is right. Don't hit him with it when he comes home. If she is agitated, he'll know she wants to talk. She should wait until later when the kids are in bed and she and her husband are settled in for the evening. Then the wife may say, "Honey, I have a problem." Note that *she* has a problem. She starts with herself and her own feelings and avoids attacking him.

She continues, "When I prepare a nice supper and it's left to get cold, I feel unappreciated." Note that there are no "yous," no attack. Her husband may get defensive and justify his repeated tardiness. She can avoid putting any pressure on him to defend by saying, "Honey, I'm sure that you have good reasons for being late. I just want to tell you how I feel."

By telling her husband that she feels unappreciated, she has introduced the fair fight issue of centricity—Am I important to you? She has also shared a feeling about it—I don't feel appreciated. And she has shared in a nonattacking manner.

Of course, the husband must be concerned about making his wife feel appreciated or important. Here is where commitment and responsibility are essential. If this is a concern to him, he will get the message that punctuality will make her feel appreciated and important. But he also may be tempted to brush this aside as an unimportant matter. If he does, his wife has another opportunity to make her point because this is the same fair fight issue. She may say, "Honey, I tried to tell you that your being late for supper makes me feel unappreciated and unimportant. And then when my feelings about that are brushed aside as unimportant, it makes me feel even more unimportant."

At this point he will see all his justifications and rationalizations as futile. He will see that a change in his behavior, not an excuse, is the only thing that will make her feel better.

This certainly is an oversimplification of the matter because sometimes it is compounded by a game on the part of the husband. It may be that he *knows* being late for supper bugs his wife and that it's a sneaky, covert way to make her angry without having to take the blame or responsibility for hurting her. This is called passive-aggressive behavior, the hardest type of behavior to deal with. It can also be classified as crazymaking.

Once the feelings about the fight issue are identified and communicated, the counselor is ready for the second step, negotiating contracts for change. There are two kinds of contracts: (1) a learning contract and (2) an action contract.

A learning contract is an agreement between a couple whereby one is told immediately when his behavior is making trouble for the other. It may seem strange that such a contract is needed, but it is.

I think, for example, of a husband who was continually putting down his wife without knowing it. She'd say something, and he'd reply, "Oh, what do you know?" He also called her "the moose" (she had a rather large nose) and "dummy" and "idiot." He put her down nonverbally with facial expressions and gestures of disgust. It came as a complete surprise that his wife felt continually put down by him; so I got them into a learning contract. Whenever he did anything to make her feel put down, she was to say, "Honey, whenever you do (or say) that, I feel put down." And he could only answer her with, "Thank you for telling me."

That last part is important—"Thank you for telling me." The tendency is to excuse or justify behavior that hurts someone else, which leads to a fight or alienation. A learning contract is a controlled way of getting a person to change behavior that is hurting someone else.

Now those words *behavior change* are the key to the rapid treatment process. If you change behavior, you'll change feelings.

The traditional approach to counseling is to change the feelings of people, but there's a better way. Change behavior that is creating bad feeling in others and you will change their feelings. When their feelings are changed, they will be disposed to change their behavior too. Consider the following diagram of the effect of behavior and feeling change:

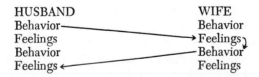

Either spouse may initiate the behavior change, or they may both initiate it. When I change my behavior and make my spouse feel pleased, she is most likely to change her behavior to please me.

The second kind of contract is an action contract—a method of getting a couple to *do* something to change their behavior. Once we have determined what behaviors are producing a bad effect, we must do something about them.

Take for example a couple who have been guilty of territorial aggression. She keeps leaving junk on his workbench in the garage. He is incensed because that workbench is his turf, and she keeps intruding. It might be a small issue, but this one action represents many encroachments on his turf, which put together are making him furious. Leaving junk on his workbench is at the head of the aggression list.

The action contract I want from her for one week—and it is specific—is to leave nothing on his workbench. This follows the two rules of an action contract. It should be *time limited* and *specific*. It is time limited so we can revise it the next week if necessary. It is specific so there is no doubt what is to be done to relieve the irritation. A third element ought to be included if possible. It is a penalty for breach of contract. This may take the form of an added obligation.

One of my clients complained that her husband never did a thing to improve the appearance of the house or yard. She wanted to rearrange the bedroom, and he wouldn't even help move the bed. He agreed that it was reasonable to help her move the bed; so he gave a date at which time it would be done. Then I said, "Suppose you don't do it? What penalty should I attach?" She cheerfully supplied the information that the backyard was high with weeds that needed to be cut. So he agreed that his penalty for not moving the bed by the deadline would incur having to cut the weeds. The bed was moved according to agreement, and a new pattern began to emerge in which he accepted at least one household chore a week.

Some counselors maintain that the only workable contract is *quid pro quo* contract—this for that. In this kind of contract the husband will agree to do certain things in exchange for the wife's doing something for him. If one fails to deliver on the contract, the other is not obligated. They use a written, signed form in this kind of agreement.

The problem I have in using this kind of contract is that the man in the aforementioned case may be getting everything he wants from his wife and may not be able to think of something of equal value he wants from her that he is not getting. There may be nothing to exchange.

If the reasonableness of the request is agreed on, I find little trouble in getting a delinquent spouse to deliver the goods without a *quid pro quo* contract.

Now I make negotiation for change sound very easy, but it isn't always. Often a spouse may agree that a request is reasonable, but when it comes right down to negotiation, he may resist and say that it is unreasonable. When we begin to talk about the unreasonableness of it, he may come up with many more feelings about their relationship that he had not voiced before. We then start the process all over to get to the root of his feelings. I may find that he not only suffers from territorial aggression, but he also suffers from centricity—he doesn't feel that he's important to his wife. Perhaps she is always running off to this meeting or that activity and never has time for him. Then I can get her into an action contract that may curtail her outside activities and get her to spend more time with him.

Negotiation for change is an important step in rapid treatment for a troubled marriage because it gives the couple something *specific to do* to remedy their situation. Unless we show them exactly how to change their behavior, it will be just so much talk. Sometimes just insight into what they are doing to each other will bring change on their own initiative, but don't count on it.

Follow-up. The final step is follow-up. Once a couple is doing well on their own, a checkup approximately four weeks after the last session should be scheduled. This is important because they may permit the situation to deteriorate and not seek help until it becomes desperate, or they may be too embarrassed to come back and admit failure. The results of that checkup will help the counselor determine if further checkups are in order.

It is also helpful to put a couple like this in a marriage enrichment or communication workshop or other therapeutic group. A number of couples whose marriages are on the mend can form a therapeutic group.

Now I have mentioned nothing of the spiritual dimension of treating the troubled marriage. With believers I integrate spiritual truth as I work with them. I use the format I have described, but it is permeated with what the Bible says about their situation. Sometimes it has to do with confession and a guilty conscience, other times with assurance.

Some Christian husbands have blown the scriptural concept of the submissive wife all out of proportion and need to be taught 1 Peter 3:7—he must share equally with his wife the good things of life because she is a co-heir in grace. And if he doesn't, his prayers will be hindered.

With unbelievers I take a different approach. I begin with the common ground of their human dilemma and my ability to intervene therapeutically. When they begin to benefit from my counseling, they are more disposed to hear what I have to say about eternal things. Before I release them from counseling, I tell them that the things I have given them will be of use only in this life, but I want to give them something of eternal value. I then present to them the claims of eternal life through Christ.

Sometimes an unsaved client will bring up the question of his spiritual condition early in counseling. This gives me an opportunity there and then to deal with his soul.

This is actually only the application of apologetics to counseling. I have gained the confidence of this person by making his marriage better. Why shouldn't he listen to the good news of eternal life in Christ? I look at it as the Nicodemus dialogue in reverse: "If I have told you of earthly things and you have believed, certainly you'll believe if I tell you of heavenly things."

NOTES

1. Charles B. Truax and Robert R. Carkhuff, *Toward Effective Counseling and Psychotherapy: Training and Practice* (Chicago: Aldine-Atherton, 1967).

2. Order from Family Life Publications, Inc., Box 427, Saluda, N.C. 28773.

3. For more information on *crazymaking*, see George Bach and Yetta M. Bernhard, *Aggression Lab: The Fair-Fight Training Manual* (Dubuque, Ia.: Kendall-Hunt, 1971), and "Crazymaking: Why You Can't Communicate with Some People," Andre Bustanoby, 13211 Overbrook Ln., Bowie, Md. 20715.

4. Order from Educational and Industrial Testing Service, P. O. Box 7234, San Diego, California 92107.

9

A Model
for Marital Therapy

DONALD F. TWEEDIE, JR.

Marital therapy has a long past and a short history. Certainly concerns for marital conflicts and efforts to mediate them have been prominent human endeavors for centuries. However, it has been in recent decades of this century that a formal field of marital therapy has developed.

One of the earlier attempts to give structure to this field is a volume edited by Bernard Green, *Psychotherapies of Marital Disharmony*.[1] He refers to the various approaches as the "Six-C's": counseling, classical, collaborative, concurrent, conjoint, and combined.

Counseling focuses on the social environment of the family. How the spouses get along, rather than their intrapsychic forces, is the primary emphasis. Green attempts to distinguish between counseling and psychotherapy, the latter being "deeper" and related to personality structural change instead of readjustment. Such a dichotomy is difficult to maintain in either theory or practice, but it

DONALD F. TWEEDIE, JR., is professor of psychology at Fuller Theological Seminary Graduate School of Psychology in Pasadena, California. He has done postdoctoral studies at Harvard Divinity School and at the University of Vienna, where he had clinical affiliation with Dr. Viktor Frankl. Dr. Tweedie is the author of numerous journal articles and papers, and has written several books, including *The Christian and Sex* and *Logotherapy*. He is married and has seven children.

is an important distinction for many involved in counseling as a technique of marital therapy.

Classical therapy is the traditional psychoanalytic approach applied to a married patient. Marital relationships are interpreted to help the patient understand the so-called transference neurosis and to overcoming resistance in therapy.

Collaborative therapy describes a situation in which each spouse is in psychoanalysis with a separate analyst. Therapists confer periodically, comparing notes and utilizing the information in the therapeutic interaction.

Concurrent therapy is that in which a husband and wife are treated during the same period of time but in separate sessions by the same therapist. Theoretically this is a very difficult and dubious psychoanalytic maneuver, but it is reported to have an initial anxiety reduction element as the couple feels a simultaneous emotional support. Concurrent therapy also tends to provide a setting of hope for the success of the marriage.

Conjoint therapy is a method in which all significant members of the conflict, including at times the whole family, are seen together by the same therapist at the same time. It is based on the theory that any behavior that occurs between two or more people is the product of everyone involved. Marital conflict is considered a nonadaptive and deteriorating process, and little regard is given to psychiatric and social diagnoses since they are considered merely different ways of labeling the problem. Conjoint therapy is an active, structured, and overtly optimistic approach to marital therapy, which is reported to be both effective and efficient in alleviating marital distress.

Green's sixth and final technique, *combined* therapy, is a mixture of the above five. He feels that some marital problems necessitate a comprehensive treatment including individual concerns, the family social setting, and relationship patterns. A variety of personnel must be available. The rationale for this treatment seems to me unconvincing, while the procedure seems unwieldy and socially unrealistic. It is more a "catch-all" than a technique. To this point conjoint therapy seems most realistic, most comprehensive, and the most likely vehicle for bringing about true marital healing.

CONTRACT THERAPY

A few years ago, I added a seventh "C"—*contract* therapy. This procedure grew out of my limited success in utilizing the various "Six C's" and a greater success in negotiating contractual agreements to help couples resolve their conflicts.

Contract therapy developed out of the frustrations I experienced counseling delinquent adolescents. During the late '60s there were a rash of referrals almost exclusively from parents, courts, or schools. These referrals rarely involved any choice on the part of the adolescent, other than a reluctant, and usually resistant, consent. After a brief period of tardy appointments most of these teenagers simply dropped out of therapy. Even when an apparently good therapeutic relationship developed, this did not seem to have any particularly lasting change upon the undesirable behavior as reported by the referral sources. John Bell's *Family Group Therapy* and Virginia Satir's *Conjoint Family Therapy*[2] led me into attempts to treat the family as a whole. Having had some success in management consultation with small corporations, I decided to use an analogue of a small corporation in trouble as a professional model. The positive progress with such an approach was gratifying.

In the next phase of development I became a more active negotiator, instead of a management analyst or a corporation consultant, and began to limit negotiation to the parents, the "offender," and the nearest age sibling. The process became more similar to the negotiation of a labor contract with the parents serving as "management" and the acting-out adolescent as "labor." I then adapted the negotiation procedure to marital conflict situations.

The general goal of contract therapy was to attain a more satisfying, cooperative, and harmonious marital pattern. This seemed most effectively accomplished by promoting the explicit self-interest of the party members. As negotiator I would help each spouse get "the best deal" possible, consonant with personal desires and the common aim.

The original contract categories were *privilege, performance,* and *penalty*. A *privilege* is any behavior that one of the parties desires but is not presently able to achieve, any behavior he presently feels compelled to continue but about which he feels negative;

or some behavior change in the spouse. A privilege is not agreed upon until the act in question is so specific that the negotiator can describe it to the satisfaction of both parties to the contract.

In *performance* the privilege-seeking person offers to exchange some behavior for his privilege.

Penalty was a secondary behavior agreement to be carried out when a party failed to perform following a privilege. However, the very negative nature of a penalty seemed to indicate that the person had not really gotten himself "a good deal." Subsequently this contract category was eliminated.

Privilege-performance pairs or dyads are the content of the contract. They are negotiated in weekly sessions, and each dyad goes into effect as soon as the process is carried out with the spouses alternating in obtaining privileges until both feel satisfied with their marriage relationship and have a "good deal."

Some of the factors that seem strategic to contract therapy are (a) not allowing private contact or communication of any of the individuals in therapy with the therapist, (b) pressure for making every desirable change in the relationship very specific, and (c) emphasizing the self-interest of the individuals in the contract construction.

During the course of the development of contract therapy, it soon came to my attention that its behavioral negotiation aspect was closely related to new movements in marital therapy that were aligned with what was called Behavior Modification.[3] A number of psychologists report models of therapy with conflicted married couples.[4]

In some ways contract therapy is similar to Behavior Modification and might, with apparent justification, be categorized with that group. It is ironic that contract therapy developed with a behavioral focus in spite of a very negative set toward "behaviorism" and with a specific existential and biblical view of man.

Some hold that the practice of a therapeutic approach is based upon the *theory* of man from which the method emerged. Since behaviorism, with its machine model of man, is the historical source of Behavior Modification, would this invalidate behavioral technology for the Christian therapist? Many would deny this. Clement, a leading researcher in Behavior Modification, asserts that one can and should distinguish between the *philosophy* of behaviorism and the methodology of behavioral science.[5] (Incidentally, in this interesting autobiographical paper, Clement presents Jesus as a leading proponent of the behavioral method called operant conditioning!) In a recent essay, Fischer has argued strongly for a distinction between "behaviorism" and "behavioralism."[6] Rybach presents a model for "existential behaviorism."[7] Apparently in spite of B. F. Skinner's thesis,[8] it is possible to use behavior modification methods and do so with both "dignity" and "freedom."

The symptom of marital conflict is the complaint system. This is the way in which spouses perceive their "bum deal" in a sick marriage. With effective negotiation in contract therapy, the system of complaints gives way to a system of satisfaction.

Contract therapy is a behavioral counseling technique developed from a biblical perspective, both with regard to the nature of man and the nature of marriage. In early stages there has been success in the mediation of marital problems. Controlled experimental studies and follow-up data are accumulating. I do not see this method as a panacea for all marriage problems but rather as a significant procedure for the clinical counselor.

Contract therapy was developed in the course of a busy clinical practice while attempting to find more efficient ways to deal with marriage and family conflict. It is a method in which the complaint systems are mediated through negotiating an explicit contract and assumes that persons dissatisfied in a relationship feel that they have been victims of a "bad deal." The healing, or therapy, of such "breakdowns" in relationship is the renegotiation of a "better deal."

The procedure involves a series of privilege-performance agreements. The therapist functions as a disinterested third-party negotiator. Each agreement provides a privilege which the privileged party believes will make the relationship more satisfactory to him. It also contains a performance of changed behavior that he is willing to exchange for the privilege. In my practice contract therapy appears to be more efficient than other modes of marital therapy.

Contract therapy has been well received in the therapeutic community, perhaps because of the simplicity of its operation and its tendency to be relatively short term. Many counselors are using at least basic aspects of it. However, it has not avoided the attention of objectors. Criticism tends to fall into two categories: It is superficial, and it is not suitable.

The first objection seems to be based upon a psychodynamic view of man, a school of thought most influenced by Freudian psychoanalysis. It assumes that personality structure is both wide and deep. Man is considered to be complex and motivated by passions beyond his conscious awareness. Conflict with others in the family circle which is critical is presumed to be an indicator of a critical intrapersonal conflict. It is therefore assumed that any successful psychotherapy must attend to the structure and unconscious dynamics of the personality. It is only with this last statement that I would take issue. The critics of contracting apparently feel that it is only momentary in its effect and perhaps dangerous in its application.

However, it is not so much direct removal of symptoms which is the focus of contract therapy, but a change of attitudes toward the symptoms which cause the symptoms to disappear. In such a case, there is no evidence to indicate that something deeper needs to be attended to or that new symptoms will appear. The existential movement has made it difficult to believe in this time-honored assumption of depth psychology.[9]

Objections to contract therapy by Christian colleagues and clients have seemed to be on two levels. The first claims that contract therapy is a neutral, and therefore a secular, method. The second goes further in seeing it as specifically non-Christian in both theory and practice. Since these objections, if true, would thwart my basic intention for a Christian approach to counseling, it is easy for me to take a defending (and probably defensive) stance. I'd like to consider these two levels in order.

It is likely true that most tools and most clinical methods are theoretically neutral in character. However, they tend never to be neutral in practice. In all cases they are to some degree expressions of the value systems of their master.

It was assumed, at least in the early history of formal clinical counseling, that a therapist could carry out his work without "contaminating" the therapy with his own personal values. This was frequently considered an asset. Clinical research has never been one of the high suits of clinical psychology, but there does seem to be a widespread agreement presently that a context of counseling is value laden.[10]

The patient presents himself as seeking values for living. Almost invariably his request is to be understood as an anxious question, What must I do to be saved? He may not even understand it as a religious question. The counselor offers himself as a professional person who has discovered for his own life vital values that are incorporated in a satisfying life style. Hanging out a shingle offering clinical services for sale is an audacious enterprise. In addition, it appears that the progress of therapy is usually gauged on the rate of identification of patient with therapist. Thus the question is not whether there will be values involved in the counseling context but rather what kind of values.

Contract therapy, as any other counseling procedure, is necessarily nonneutral. In action it will tend to reflect the value system of the therapist. Negotiations will be limited to those behaviors which are appropriate from my point of view, that is, those which do not violate Christian ethics. And, on the positive side, the therapist may promote privilege-performance agreements such as going to church, reading the Bible, engaging in devotional exercises, or taking the mote out of one's own eye, which are generally construed as appropriate Christian behaviors.

The second level of objection is not whether contract therapy could be neutral but whether, in fact, it carries basic values contrary to a Christian life-view. These criticisms come under two general heads: Contract therapy attempts to impose law upon a relationship rather than to introduce grace; and it appeals to personal privilege and caters to personal self-interest in a way that is contrary to Christian ethics, in which one should not "set his own advantage as his objective" (1 Cor. 10:24, Phillips).

The relationship of law and grace is a difficult matter, whether in psychology or theology. It is superficially easier to keep them separated and dichotomized than to keep them in a dialectic, in a life process. Yet the latter seems to be where a self-revealing, covenanting God would put them. Christ talks about grace fulfilling the law rather than abrogating it. Law without grace is bondage; grace without law is capricious, and perhaps even vicious.

This last sentence sounded so stark that I felt the need to pause and telephone a theologian friend for counsel. He assured me that a biblical theology worthy of the name would give ready assent. He said that faith always carries imperatives. It appears that no biblical covenant, from Noah to Christ, could be divorced from responsibilities interacting with a gracious offer.

Thus the mediating of a "better covenant" in marital therapy, instead of being non-Christian, is more likely to provide an atmosphere of gracious relationship that comports well with the gospel. The precarious, though precious, passage between the Charybdis of licentious "cheap grace" and the Scylla of legalism is important for both theologians and psychologists. God provided the law first so that grace could both abound and be appreciated. Contract therapy tried to emulate this procedure.

The second Christian concern about contract therapy is that it engenders selfishness and special pleading. Certainly a Christian counselor should hesitate to promote these. It is true that to negotiate a privilege is to arrange a special advantage for the complainer. However, he performs in such a way as to provide adequate consideration for his spouse in every transaction. Each privilege-performance agreement serves to make a more satisfying marital covenant.

The reason that we have no obvious analogue for renegotiation in the gospel covenant is due to the character of the offer. A gracious God offers salvation in a satisfying and meaningful life, and the relatively small consideration requested of us obviates complaint. Only God has grounds for complaint. The offer of gold for ashes is hardly a basis for dissatisfaction to the recipient of the offer.

The cultivation of a "second mile" attitude, or a "coat and cloak too" set, is an important goal of Christian counseling, but not, in my experience, a very useful initial intervention in marital and familial conflict. The person who feels that he has "been had" is already troubled with a "martyr complex." In terms of psychological dynamics, it may well be observed that "turning the other cheek" is no more a willing acquiescence to an unfair demand than is a counterattack. It really is a forthright request for a "better deal" in relationship, risky, but having long-range self-interest.

However, there were developmental problems in both the "name and the game" of contract therapy. The "penalty" phase of the contracting became more a liability than an asset. It was a negative way to patch up a poorly negotiated privilege-performance agreement.

The name *contract* and the process of "contracting" became the most important problem areas. They often drew resistance in therapy because of their negative emotional character which was perceived as sterile and impersonal—a way to buy a house or a car, perhaps, but hardly the thing to do in a fractured relationship. One doesn't "buy back" satisfaction in marriage! The procedure, once beyond this roadblock, was effective, but it was often a very high hurdle. I began to believe that a rose by any other name might not smell as sweet. Call it a skunk cabbage, and it will start to have a peculiar odor.

COVENANT THERAPY

Some three years ago I had started to use the term *covenant* as an alternative synonym for a contract. I liked the flavor of it and noted that it drew less resistance. I thought it best just to use it as an alternative since *contract* was the identifying nomenclature and change would be resisted. When I subsequently discovered that I had difficulty remembering what Kareem Abdul-Jabbar used to be called, I decided that change is quite easily accepted.

I was amazed at the differential of the two words. A theoretical dissertation in pastoral care was written, discriminating the "two procedures" that I considered identical![11] The author decided covenant was the best method, and I was inclined to agree. Covenant therapy was deemed to be more "Godlike," gracious, and personal.

There is an etymological advantage also. Covenant therapy assumes that all divine and human relationships and interactions may be expressed as facets of a covenant, an interpersonal agreement. Most covenants are implicit and covert; others, as in the case of legal covenants, usually called contracts, are explicit and overt.

Most personal covenants change over time, and the parties may not be aware of the changes. The covenant of marriage is often an implicit agreement to perpetuate the pleasure of courtship, cemented by sexual privilege. It is rarely designed to cover the exigencies related to the less present problems of "life together." Family covenants, like topsy, usually just grow.

Every human interaction may be specified as a covenant relationship, and every change, as a covenantal modification. Every affirming of relationship is a covenant renewal. Covenanting is a way of life. Most people in distress desire better covenants with the important people in their lives. The following brief account will indicate the typical pattern of covenant therapy.

The couple requested therapy for a very conflicted and unsatisfactory marriage. The husband had been having an affair over a period of several months with his secretary and had finally left home for a brief time to live with this girl. The wife was acutely depressed and very discouraged about the prospect of the marriage surviving. The husband expressed his love and concern for their three children as a ground for his returning home. In addition to this third-party problem, the couple presented a variety of conflict areas, especially with reference to their religious behavior. Both were from a Roman Catholic communion, and the wife felt unable to be active in church attendance inasmuch as she felt estranged from the church by her regular use of oral contraceptives.

In spite of a moderate amount of reluctance to use behavior rather than feelings as the focus of therapy, they rather quickly became involved. There was also initial difficulty in getting the wife to move from general privileges such as love, concern, patience, and respect to specific instances of these attitudes in action.

The following are the series of agreements that were incorporated into the final signed covenant: (1) She requested as the first privilege that he would see that the children's seatbelts were fastened each time before they went on a family drive. She in turn agreed to make no negative comments about his driving. (2) He requested "solitude times." These became defined as the time from 7:00 to 8:00 P.M. on Mondays, Wednesdays, and Thursdays in which he could be by himself at the poolside behind their home or at a nearby golf driving range. In exchange he would participate in three weekly "talk times." They were to be from 10:00 to 10:30 P.M. on Tuesdays, Thursdays, and Sundays. (3) The wife also wanted him to open the car door for her and to help her with her wrap when they would be out in public. In return he joined the company bowling league, with the proviso that she could accompany him when she wished. (4) The husband requested that she would not again mention the affair in which he had been involved or the name of the girl. For this privilege, he would take her out to dinner weekly. She would decide whether alone or with the children. (5) He also requested that she would accompany him and the children to church regularly. His performance was to assist in several specified household tasks.

After four sessions, the wife's depression lifted, and both spouses became hopeful and helpful in the covenanting. The defensive aspect of agreement changed to mutual cooperation. The above were the provisions of the finalized covenant. They were seen for a total of ten sessions. Subsequent follow-ups of three months, one year, and two years report a high level of enjoyment and satisfaction in the marriage.

Covenant therapy is a process whereby the relationship of two or more persons which has become pathological and/or nonfunctional is treated through attaining and experiencing an explicit, mutually agreed upon, and satisfactory relational covenant, mediated through the services of a third person.

Covenant therapy involves both the attainment and the experiencing of a better covenant. The former is obtained through agreements of privilege-performance, the latter through validation in life of whether these agreements work. The covenant must be explicit so that each party understands precisely what he offers, what he expects, what the consideration for the offer *is* in precise detail. These dyads of privilege and performance change the system of behavior and stimulate positive attitude changes, which in turn bring about health and satisfaction to the marital relationship. Covenant therapy, as developed to this point, is radically conjoint, radically behavioral, and based upon a radically biblical model of man.

NOTES

1. Bernard Green, *Psychotherapies of Marital Disharmony* (New York: Free Press, 1965).

2. John Bell, *Family Group Therapy* (1961); Virginia Satir, *Conjoint Family Therapy* (Palo Alto, Cal.: Science Behavior Books, 1964).

3. D. Tweedie, "Contract Therapy and Behavior Modification," *Journal of Psychology and Theology* 1 (1973): 50–56.

4. R. Stuart, "Operant-Interpersonal Treatment for Marital Discord," *Journal of Consulting and Clinical Psychology* 33 (1969): 675–82; R. Liberman, "Behavioral Approaches to Family and Couple Therapy," *American Journal of Orthopsychiatry* 40 (1970): 106–18; R. Weis, H. Hops, and G. Patterson, "A framework for conceptualizing marital conflict, technology for altering it, some data for evaluating it," in L. A. Hamerlynck, et al., eds., *Behavior Change—Methodology, Concepts and Practice: Proceedings* (Champaign, Ill.: Research Press, 1973); A. Rappaport and J. Harrell, "A Behavioral-Exchange Model for Marital Counseling," *Family Coordinator* 21 (1972): 203–12.

5. P. Clement, "Can a Christian Be a Behaviorist?" in H. N. Maloney, ed., *The Psychologist Christian*, forthcoming.

6. C. Fischer, "Behaviorism and Behavioralism," *Psychotherapy* 10 (1973): 2–4.

7. D. Rybach, "A Vector Model for Existential Behaviorism," *Psychotherapy* 10 (1973): 5–9; see also D. Tweedie, "Should We Behave Ourselves?" *Cross-Talk* 3:1.

8. B. F. Skinner, *Beyond Freedom and Dignity* (New York: Alfred Knopf, 1971).

9. D. Tweedie, *Logotherapy*, 3rd ed (Grand Rapids, Mich.: Baker Book House, 1973).

10. C. Buhler, *Values in Psychotherapy* (New York: Free Press, 1962).

11. M. Lum, "An Examination of the Concepts of Covenant and Contract in Marital Counseling" (Ph.D. diss.), Fuller Seminary, 1974.

10

Training Christian Couples for Marriage Counseling

NORMAN G. WAKEFIELD

"Competent Counselors Urgently Needed." This headline appeared recently in a family life publication. It reflects the awareness of a need of significant importance. Not only is there a need for professional counselors, but perhaps an even greater need exists for trained lay counselors who can provide assistance for those who do not have the financial resources for, in-depth need of, or access to a professional counselor. Perhaps if the church devoted more of its time and resources to discover, train, and utilize lay persons for counseling, it would reduce the heavy load placed upon the pastoral staff.

In marriage seminars we ask participants to discuss their agreement or disagreement with the following statement: "Every couple should have friends with whom they can talk over their marital problems and adjustments." As we listen in on their discussions, inevitably someone will share a personal illustration of how his or her marriage was enriched through another couple's counsel. Often the counsel stems from insight that the counseling couple has

NORMAN G. WAKEFIELD is associate professor of Christian Education at Talbot Theological Seminary in La Mirada, California, and codirector of Christian Marriage Enrichment Seminars (CMES). Previously he served as Christian Education director and consultant for churches in Virginia and Kentucky. With CMES he travels widely to lead marriage and family seminars. Dr. Wakefield is married and has five children.

gained in their own marriage. We know that the potential for certain couples to assist other couples does exist.

My intent is to explore the possibility of using Christian couples for marriage counseling. An underlying assumption is that trained Christian couples can function effectively in a counseling role. This is not to imply that a lay couple can handle all counseling problems. Even professionally trained counselors practice referral for clients whose need is beyond their expertise. But with a plan for referral, the trained Christian couple can function in a marriage counseling ministry.

Many churches do have lay couples available for training. One Christian layman who has an outstanding counseling ministry wrote the following in personal correspondence:

> Surely the door for lay counseling within the church is wide open and the talent available. . . . to my notion, the availability of talent isn't the problem; rather, the general program of the "normal" evangelical church is too narrow and doesn't normally include an emphasis on developing family life in the church.

WHY SHOULD COUPLES DO MARRIAGE COUNSELING?

Why should the church consider training Christian couples to do marriage counseling? First, many pastors find themselves too busy with other demands of the ministry to provide adequate premarital and marital counseling. When we recommend five or six sessions of premarital counseling for each couple, some pastors say, "I could never find enough time to fit in five sessions." They are often so busy fulfilling other ministries that they do not have ample time for counseling.

Second, some evidence suggests that trained, carefully chosen lay people may be able to function as well in marriage counseling as the professional counselor. The Marriage Guidance Movement in England utilized both trained lay counselors and professional counselors. The evaluation of the psychiatric supervisors was that the lay counselors functioned as effectively as the professionals.[1] This is in harmony with the evaluation of the noted psychologist Carl R. Rogers, whose personal experience led him to the following conclusion:

In our courses we have had students from the fields of education, theology, industrial relations, nursing, and students with inter-disciplinary training. It has been quite impossible to see any signifi-cant differences in the rate at which such students become therapists. It would seem that the orientation to personal relationships with which they enter a training program is more important than the specific course work they have had or the scientific knowledge they possess.[2]

One should not minimize the value of thorough psychological training; neither should one discredit the potential of gifted indi-viduals.

A third reason that Christian couples should be considered rests in the fact that Christians have recognized that spiritual gifts have been distributed throughout the body of Christ for ministry to the members of the body (1 Cor. 12). Certain gifts appear to be re-lated to the counseling ministry. This would suggest that an indi-vidual might not have received formal training as a counselor but does possess spiritual sensitivity to human needs and solutions. Thus, those Christian couples who demonstrate spiritual maturity, insight into marital needs, and a warm, caring spirit should be equipped with counseling skills which enable them to minister to other couples. The fact that some form of this ministry is occurring demonstrates its larger possibility. One gifted counselor has written:

Most of my training and study has been on my own and through actual counseling situations. It almost seems as if I came in the back door or rather started in reverse. Most seem to be trained, at least in part, and then sent out, but not in my case. Surely, God has been very gracious. Some have suggested, and I agree in part, that I have a measure of spiritual giftedness, or natural ability.[3]

Gifted and/or well-trained lay people already exist in many churches. Is it not unfortunate that we do not take advantage of this human resource in ministering to the body of Christ? Many people feel more comfortable sharing difficulties with persons when they have observed a consistent Christian maturity in that person's life.

WHO SHOULD BE SELECTED?

Two essential ingredients contained in an effective couple's counseling program are careful selection and thorough training. At the heart of selection is the ability to identify those couples who have a testimony of Christian character which is consistently observed. To select individuals who are spiritual novices or struggling in their own marriage would certainly be unwise.

The following suggestions serve as clues for finding couples to train. To begin with, look for couples who are already being sought out for assistance. Usually at least one such couple can be found in a church. The fact that others are reaching out to them indicates that others see something in them that they find helpful. Usually such individuals are being sought out because they demonstrate a hospitable, caring spirit.

One should also be alert for individuals who have had previous training in marriage counseling, psychology, human relations, or related disciplines. The person may be functioning in such positions as a guidance counselor in a high school, personnel supervisor in a local industry, or a physician in private practice. These persons have already developed helping skills. When working as a husband-wife team they often can effectively devote their counseling skills to marital relationships.

In some situations a person with a basic college education can qualify for short-termed specialized training. For example, for the past several years Talbot Theological Seminary has offered a two-week summer school course in premarital and marital counseling. Such training would be of invaluable help to a Christian couple preparing for a counseling ministry to other couples. An alert pastor might direct a couple into such a training program and then begin to work with them in a supervisory manner as they counseled other couples.

When selecting couples for training in marriage counseling, one should also endeavor to identify those who manifest a natural or spiritual giftedness toward helping others solve their problems. Such individuals may have had little or no formal training, yet reflect the ability to excel in a helping relationship. A loving mother, for example, who has diligently led her daughters in preparing for marriage may have much training and insight available to share with other young ladies (Titus 2:4).

Couples who are being considered for training will be more effective if they possess insight into biblical principles of marriage, human relations, and personal growth. While a plan of directed reading, cassette tapes, and seminars can enrich this area, those who already demonstrate skill in counseling are more likely candidates for selection.

The careful selection of the right Christian couple is a key to an effective marriage counseling ministry. It is wise to discern prayerfully which couples should be candidates for training rather than hastily gather together anyone who will come. At times the church has come under attack for having inadequately trained persons functioning in important roles.

HOW CAN THE COUPLE BE TRAINED?

For an effective counseling ministry, thorough training is crucial. Such training will assure a solid foundation. It will also create the basis for a unified philosophy of ministry. Training helps avoid a superficial program and stresses the importance of the task to the counselors.

In this section my intention is not to describe one method of training couples but rather to identify a number of resources, programs, or techniques which can be incorporated into the training. To some extent the training program must be designed according to the strengths and needs of the couple being trained and according to the way the couple will be utilized in the marriage counseling program. For example, if the couple's primary responsibilities rest upon preventive premarital counseling, the emphasis of their training will differ from the couple who mainly focuses on *corrective* counseling for married couples.

In the creation of an actual training program one should draw together those resources and learning experiences which are appropriate for his objective, available, and economically or practically feasible. Thus, none of the ideas suggested below are intended to be used in isolation.

Premarital and marital counselor training tapes. The cassette series *Upon This Foundation, Vol. 1* is a series of six tapes designed to provide counselor training in premarital counseling. An accompanying handbook makes the kit especially helpful as a study program. The tapes provide clear, practical instruction in how to conduct six sessions of premarital counseling. Suggestions for materials that should be used with the couple are included with the handbook, as well as bibliographic resources which the counselor can use for assigned reading with the couple preparing for marriage.

If the pastor of a church were training couples to do premarital counseling, these tapes would be invaluable as a basis for his training program. The tapes also cover principles and resources for group preparation counseling.

Training programs. Another means to train couples is through professionally developed training seminars which help equip the counselor with skills and resources for counseling. The Peer-Counseling Program developed by the Link-Care Foundation is designed to give the layman both counseling theory and practice. The trainee receives in-depth instruction at the foundation and ongoing supervision as long as the counselor remains active in the program. The professional supervisor maintains a consultative-instructive relationship with the counselor after he returns to his local church.

Whereas the Peer-Counseling Program focuses on the development of counseling skills in general, the Christian Marriage Enrichment Seminar (CMES) provides training for church staff members and lay couples in areas of marital and premarital enrichment. If counseling is seen as both preventive as well as corrective, then CMES provides valuable couple counseling training.

CMES is an intensive two-day seminar which endeavors to combine helpful instruction and a creative learning process. In this way the couple is involved in counseling/learning experiences which they can employ with couples in their own church. Many resources and evaluative tools are provided which focus on the communication process, goal setting, conflict resolution, husband-wife roles, and so on. CMES training is especially profitable for couples who would be involved in leading couples groups, retreats, or seminars for marital growth.

A third type of training program is that which a pastor or competent church leader might institute within the local church. In *Group Counseling in the Church,*[4] John Oman describes a counseling program he has conducted for many years within his church.

While the focus is upon group counseling rather than marriage counseling, Oman has trained lay persons to lead group counseling sessions.

Pastor-couple internship. The pastor may choose to work with one couple at a time, training them through an internship with him. He begins by selecting the most suitable couple (or couples if he feels that he can work with more than one couple) and spending time with them in instruction and skill development. He will likely assign directed reading or cassette tapes for homework. Once he feels that they have developed a level of proficiency to undertake marriage counseling, he moves to a supportive, supervising role in which he assists them in problem situations or in enriching their skills and knowledge.

Cooperative training approach. Within a metropolitan area another approach is possible. Several churches could sponsor couple training under the direction of a highly trained counselor. Since the need for training-supervision is great, churches should explore the possibility of seeking out a professional Christian marriage counselor. He could undertake a training program and supervise a multichurch couple-counseling ministry which would provide ongoing, supportive assistance to couples doing the marriage counseling. This would also provide a referral basis for persons who needed more in-depth assistance.

IN WHAT WAYS CAN THE COUPLE BE USED?

Several avenues can be explored in utilizing couples for marriage counseling. The church leadership will likely consider its needy areas and endeavor to train couples to minister in those situations. Different couples with their unique giftedness, training, or expertise can be used in various ways.

Premarital counseling is one extremely needy area in which counseling couples should be used. Training materials have already been described which do much to equip a couple with what to include and how to counsel. One Roman Catholic priest has trained numerous couples to conduct premarital counseling.

Dr. Robert Wheatley, pastor of Boulevard Park Presbyterian Church in Seattle, Washington, has trained four couples to do premarital counseling in his church. He requires six sessions of counseling for each couple being married. The first and last sessions are conducted by the pastor; the second through the fifth, by the counseling couple. The counseling sessions led by the couple focus on such areas as financial matters, roles, how to handle quarrels and problems, and sexual aspects. Counseling couples have been selected from among mature Christians who have demonstrated a keen interest in family life. Supplemental training has been provided through a training seminar outside the church.

One of the benefits which Dr. Wheatley cited was that hospitality is built into this approach since the counselors invite the couple into their home. The couple to be married sees a Christian home "in operation." This also seems to build a quality relationship that encourages the couple to come for assistance if later problems arise following marriage. The pastor has found this approach to premarital counseling to be very effective. Both the counseling couples and the couples being counseled have been enthusiastic about the value of this plan.

Another church in Santa Ana, California, has trained couples to counsel newlyweds. The pastoral staff provides the basic premarital counseling. When the couple is united in marriage a trained, mature Christian couple is assigned to provide counseling and guidance as the marriage relationship develops. A member of the pastoral staff reports that this has provided a very helpful ministry to couples.

In the above situation a three-dimensional training approach has been used. First, the couple attended the Christian Marriage Enrichment Seminar. Second, a member of the pastoral staff met weekly with the couple for training. Third, a study program of books and cassette tapes was utilized. Through this means the counseling couple has enriched their insight into marriage counseling and has grown in their counseling skill.

The situations described above underscore the importance and value of a team relationship between the pastoral staff and the counseling couple. For one thing, the pastor can provide ongoing training appropriate to the counseling couple's needs. In addition, the pastor can receive feedback which helps keep him acquainted with the progress of those being counseled. The team approach also avoids the danger of the counseling couple's ministry becoming isolated and unsupervised. Whenever possible couples who do marriage counseling should become integrated into a larger team ministry for the welfare of all involved.

Another way in which the counseling couple can minister is through what is termed "family growth groups," or "family clusters." In this setting the counseling couple functions as a shepherd/counselor team for a nucleus of couples or family units seeking to work out marital problems or enrich their family relationships. Such an arrangement might be designed around group counseling of those with related needs or around couple counseling with supplementary contacts with other families for fellowship. This can be especially helpful to one-parent families in which both counseling and support are needed.

In some situations the couple's counseling ministry flows out of a Sunday school class or Bible study group which they lead. One counseling layman writes:

> Approximately eight years ago, I began leading small group Bible studies among high school students. In the course of events, I began informally counseling with some of them as well as referred friends. . . . (I) decided to focus more on "problem parents" than on "problem kids." The more time I spent with the "problem parents," the more convinced I was that an even greater ministry was available.[5]

This individual has developed an active counseling ministry which has been of help to many Christians and non-Christians.

Often by utilizing competent couples in teaching classes on marriage and family, needy persons seek out the counseling couple's assistance. Another avenue of ministry is through training couples to lead premarital, marital, or family seminars and retreats. Though such situations might not be thought of in the context of counseling, usually much insight can be given and personal counsel often follows when these relevant areas are explored. It has been my experience that those who share in marriage seminars inevitably are sought out afterwards for personalized assistance.

The pastor who is seeking assistance in his marriage counseling ministry should not overlook those who have strengths in special areas. These persons can be utilized for *supplemental counseling*. For example, one couple might counsel couples who need guidance in financial and budget matters. Another couple may have excellent insight in child-rearing or communication. While these persons might not be available or qualified for a larger ministry of couple counseling, they can serve on a referral basis for special situations.

CAUTIONS AND CHALLENGES

This chapter does not intend to treat lightly the importance of highly trained counselors. It is strongly recommended that no couple counseling ministry be developed which will lead to amateurish, incompetent counseling. Those implementing a program should adopt high standards with ongoing training and supervision. Care should be exercised to follow any local or state regulations.

I have attempted to explore creative alternatives to traditional forms of marriage counseling within the church. When carefully undertaken and wisely supervised, the use of Christian couples to do marriage counseling has much to commend itself. The opportunity is ripe for qualified individuals to demonstrate models whereby this can be implemented on a larger scale.

NOTES

1. John W. Drakeford, *Counseling for Church Leaders* (Nashville, Tenn.: Broadman Press, 1961), p. 26.

2. Carl Rogers, *Client-Centered Therapy* (Boston: Houghton Mifflin, 1951), pp. 435–36.

3. From my personal correspondence.

4. John Oman, *Group Counseling in the Church: A Practical Guide for Lay Counselors* (Minneapolis: Augsburg, 1972).

5. From my personal correspondence.

II

The Church
and Marriage Enrichment

H. NORMAN WRIGHT

The romantic veneer of marriage and family life has been discarded during the past fifty years. Problems which have existed for many years have surfaced, and the entire nation is aware of family stress. In the Report on the American Family by *Better Homes and Gardens*, 71 percent of the over three hundred thousand participants felt that "American family life is in trouble."[1] Twenty-five hundred professional family educators and marriage counselors participating in the National Alliance for Family Life Research said, "There is a definite need for strengthening family life in this nation at the present time."[2]

Not only are changes seen in the type of family structure but in the permanency and longevity of the institution of marriage itself. In 1870 there were 27 divorces for every 1000 marriages in the United States. In 1972 there were 455 for every 1000.[3] In November 1974, an article in the *Los Angeles Times* reported that in Orange County, California, during the first six months of 1974 there

H. NORMAN WRIGHT is associate professor of psychology at Biola College, La Mirada, California, and has taught at Talbot Theological Seminary, Rosemead Graduate School of Psychology, and Fuller Theological Seminary. He is licensed in California as a marriage, child and family counselor, and has been involved in private practice for a number of years. He is the author of several Sunday school curricula and a number of books, including *Christian Marriage and Family Relations,* and *The Living Marriage.* Mr. Wright and his wife Joyce have two children.

were 6,372 marriages and 6,702 divorces. In a recent cartoon in the *Los Angeles Times* a pastor was performing a wedding. As he stood before the couple and completed the ceremony, he replaced the usual "Till death do you part" with "Till divorce do you part." Is this unreal? Alvin Toffler considered this question in *Future Shock:* "As conventional marriage proves itself less and less capable of delivering on its promise of lifelong love, therefore, we can anticipate open public acceptance of temporary marriages."[4] One has suggested "an apprentice period for people contemplating marriage, a five year terminal point for all marriages with the option of either renewal or cancellation of the contract, and specially trained, government financed substitute parents for the children of dissolved marriages." Another alternative is a "two level system with the first level of marriage limited to a five year period with no children allowed and then either cancellation of the contract or renewal to a permanent non-dissolvable relationship and children allowed"![5]

Dr. Carl Rogers in *Becoming Partners: Marriage and Its Alternatives* said:

> To me it seems that we are living in an important and uncertain age, and the institution of marriage is most assuredly in an uncertain state. If 50 to 75 percent of Ford or General Motors cars completely fell apart within the early part of their lifetimes as automobiles, drastic steps would be taken. We have no such well-organized way of dealing with our social institutions, so people are groping, more or less blindly, to find alternatives to marriage (which is certainly *less* than 50 percent successful). Living together without marriage, living in communes, extensive childcare centers, serial monogamy (with one divorce after another), the women's liberation movement to establish the woman as a person in her own right, new divorce laws which do away with the concept of guilt—these are all gropings toward some new form of man-woman relationship for the future. It would take a bolder man than I to predict what will emerge.[6]

The problem is not with the institution of marriage itself. The problem centers with the individuals within that structure and their attitudes. As Richard Lessor wrote,

> In the 20th century, it is not a matter of marriage having been tried and found wanting. Marriage is deeply wanted but largely untried.

Today in place of exerting consistent effort and determination to make one's marriage work the solution is to "bail out."[7]

Not only are families of today disrupted by divorce, but there are other means of dissolving relationships as well.

According to the Federal Bureau of Investigation Statistics, police across the nation receive more calls for family conflicts than for murders, aggravated batteries and all other serious crimes. The category of family conflicts includes not only quarrels between husband and wife but also between parent and child.[8]

FBI statistics report that "over 50 percent of all homicides committed are attacks by one member of a family upon another member of the same family."[9]

Not only does this terrify families, but law enforcement officials are reacting as well.

In general, police don't like dealing with family quarrels because they don't know what to expect and frequently the calls prove to be dangerous. FBI statistics show that 22 percent of all police fatalities occur while investigating domestic disturbances.[10]

These events and transitions are bound to have some effect upon people in our society. Nathan Ackerman, a leading family psychiatrist, expressed it this way:

At present, anxiety about marriage and family is almost universal. On every hand, one sees nervous concern over teenage marriage, infidelity, divorce, loosening sex standards, women's lib, momism, the decline of parental authority, the anarchy of youth, and so on. One senses deepening disillusion—even despair—surrounding the value of family life.[11]

The ultimate depth of pessimism is seen in the words of Nathan Ackerman concerning the family situation:

I am a psychiatrist who has devoted a lifetime to studying emotional problems of family living. I have pioneered in the field of family therapy. From where I sit, the picture of marriage and family in present-day society is a gloomy one. Family life seems to be cracking at the seams, and an effective mortar is nowhere available.[12]

There is, however, an effective mortar: the person of Jesus Christ. The presence of Christ, the ministry of the Holy Spirit, and intense effort and work dedicated to the application of Scripture can bring stability, growth, and mutual satisfaction into a marital relationship.

What can a local church do to minister in such a manner that lives are actually changed? A pattern and procedure can be implemented to formulate a meaningful ministry.

A step involved in the enrichment of married life is to ask, What are you trying to accomplish? What is your goal? Is your ministry prevention? Or is it reconstruction? Or both? No matter how the objective is stated, one fact must be emphasized: In order to change marriages, build the family, or prepare people for married life, we must work with *individuals,* for marriage is composed of individuals. A marriage in trouble is composed of individuals in trouble, especially as they interact with each other. The thrust must be twofold: Helping individuals to grow in maturity and helping them adjust to being married partners. Unfortunately some churches assume that the latter portion of this objective will emerge *naturally* if the first part is achieved. It does not appear to happen naturally.

Specifically a goal is to help individuals with their attitudes and behavior so they will become motivated to change themselves (and not others) and begin to live the Christian life in the closest, most intimate of all personal relationships. *The goal is mature Christians (individuals) who can follow the biblical pattern of living in their family life.* This maturity is described in Galatians 5:22–23: "But the fruit of the Spirit is love, joy, peace, patience, kindness, goodness, faithfulness, gentleness, self-control; against such there is no law."

Over the years research has discovered various characteristics which are evident in successful marriages. These "marriageability traits," as they are called, should be specific goals that individuals work toward as they are assisted by the church's ministry. Some of these traits are as follows:

Adaptability and flexibility are necessary ingredients in a successful marriage. A person must be able to adjust to change with a minimum of rigidity. One must be able to accept and adapt to the ways in which a partner is different from oneself; one must be able and willing to work toward a different life style if necessary.

Empathy is a positive characteristic necessary for all interpersonal relationships, but even more so for marriage. It is the ability to be sensitive to the needs, hurts, and desires of others, feeling with them and experiencing their world with them from their perspective. If they hurt, we hurt. If they are excited, we can be excited with them and understand their feeling response.

A third marriageability trait is the ability to work through problems. Problems, conflicts, and differences are part and parcel of marriage. Couples who accept and properly dispel and control their emotional reactions, who clarify and define their problems, and work together toward solutions will in all likelihood remain married.

The ability to give and receive love is a necessary trait. Giving love involves more than verbalizing. It must also be evident in tangible ways that both partners recognize. Behavior, actions, and attitudes convey this in a meaningful manner, but just as important is the ability to accept love from another. Some people have such a need to be needed that they feel fulfilled by giving. To receive and accept love threatens them and, in their own eyes, lowers their self-worth. If one partner continues to be unable to accept love, usually the other partner will give up or will find someone else who will accept his or her love.

Emotional stability—accepting one's emotions and controlling them—lends balance to a relationship. We depend upon a person who has a consistent, dependable, emotional response. Extreme flare-ups and decisions based upon emotional response do not lend themselves to stable relationships.

The goal also includes assisting couples to understand, accept, and implement the meaning of marriage as expressed in this definition:

A Christian marriage is a total commitment of two people to the person of Jesus Christ and to each other. It is a commitment in which there is no holding back of anything. A Christian marriage is similar to a solvent, a freeing of the man and woman to be themselves and become all that God intends for them to become.

Marriage is the refining process that God will use to have us develop into the man or woman he wants us to be.

Perhaps another goal would be to assist couples in undertaking and applying the following scriptural patterns of responsibility to their lives.

GENERAL PARENTAL DUTY

Be an Example	1 Kings 9:4; 2 Chron. 17:3
To Teach	Deut. 6:7; 4:9; 31:13; Prov. 4:3, 4; Exod. 12:14, 26–27; Prov. 1:8
To Train	Prov. 22:6
To Provide For	2 Cor. 12:14
To Nurture	Eph. 6:4
To Control	1 Tim. 3:4
To Love	Titus 2:4
To Correct	Prov. 13:24; 19:18; 22:15; 22:13

FATHER'S DUTY

To Rule	1 Tim. 3:12; 3:4
To Chasten	Prov. 19:18
To Correct	Prov. 22:15; 23:13
To Teach	Deut. 6:7; 11:18–21; 4:9–10; Prov. 4:1–4; 1:8
To Nurture; Not to Provoke	Eph. 6:4; Col. 3:21
To Provide For	1 Tim. 5:8; 2 Cor. 12:14
To Encourage	1 Thess. 2:11
To Command	Gen. 18:19
To Tell	Exod. 10:2
To Guide	Jer. 3:4
To Discipline	Prov. 3:12; Heb. 12:6

MOTHER'S DUTY

To Correct	Prov. 29:15
To Have Compassion	Isa. 49:15
To Comfort	Isa. 66:13
To Love	Titus 2:4
To Teach	Prov. 1:8; 31:26
To Be Gentle	1 Thess. 2:7
To Be Kind	Prov. 31:26

A major step after setting goals is determining how to motivate people. We must minister to three basic types of individuals: those who are complacent and feel there is nothing which needs to be improved within the marriage or family relationship; those who know there are problems but refuse to deal with them; and those who are aware of problems and are seeking solutions.

Those in the first two classifications might be considered to have hardened their hearts. There is a self-righteousness about them. Others need to change but not themselves. This is also the group that would answer in the negative to Jesus' question in John 5, asked of the man at the pool, "Do you want to be healed? Do you really want to change?" The *last group*, however, *would* answer yes to this question.

How then does one motivate and minister to each of the three classes? Through preaching and exhortation? Through teaching which tells them what they should be doing? A typical result of this approach is to elicit resistance from the first group, and unfortunately the second group feels the message applies only to the other family members and not themselves.

The last group feels even more guilty for they are *already aware* that something must be done. They need to be given hope that change and a new pattern of life is possible, and they need to be shown step by step how to move toward the positive life style. Preaching and teaching which does this and considers the principles of change *will* be effective.

To bring about change for all three groups of individuals, several principles should be considered. These are presented best by Martha Leypoldt in her book *Learning Is Change.* An individual is ready to learn or change when or if any of the following occur.

1. In a time of conflict. When one is faced with conflict he must make a choice and feel there is a potential for change.
2. When there is a feeling of inadequacy. Most people do not want to feel inadequate and at this point they may be ready to learn.
3. When a need or problem is recognized. When a person faces a crisis he usually is willing to seek help and thus there is a potential for change.
4. When a goal is set. When this occurs it is a high probability learning situation.
5. Searching for meaning in life. This again is a time for change. If these five principles are true, why don't we use them more in helping people move forward in their Christian walk? There are

times when people move into these situations naturally, and there are times when *we can help structure* these conditions.

One of the most effective means is to help create a feeling of unrest within the individual. One way of accomplishing this is to have a person make a value judgment or evaluation concerning his or her family life or marriage. The following questions have been used successfully in sessions with married couples. Those present give their own written responses and later share them with their spouses.

1. If you were to describe your marriage with one word, what would the word be?
2. What are the strengths in your marriage?
3. How do you think your spouse would describe your marriage?
4. What do you feel is the weakest area in your marriage?
5. What specifically will you do this week to enrich your marriage?

Another means of using some of the principles for change has been the formulation of a step-by-step procedure for applying the Scripture to one's life. This takes time and is best used with one passage of Scripture or one single concept which is presented first. The step-by-step process is presented verbally or with an overhead projector, and time is given so that each person can write down his or her response to every question. Often after answering all the questions, people share their responses in small groups and close their time together with prayer. The following questions are a sample of how this procedure might be carried out using Psalm 119:9–11 as the basic passage.

1. Am I satisfied with this area of my life?
2. What are the consequences of not following this teaching?
3. What are the consequences of doing what it says?
4. How do you see yourself doing this? Give practical examples.
5. When will you start doing this?
6. Pray and do it in the strength of Christ and believe that it is possible. Don't say, "I can't do it." Maybe you have never

learned how and now you can. Refer to Philippians 4:13 and Jeremiah 33:3.

7. Memorize the passage of Scripture you are working on (Ps. 119:9–11).

In addition to these principles another factor must be considered. One does not bring about as much change in large groups as in small groups. We normally measure success and effectiveness by numbers. A large class of one hundred or even fifteen thousand in some programs may attract people, but the difficulty lies in affecting lasting application. Changes in knowledge and information may occur (although at times this too is questionable!) especially with proper methods and visual aids, but changes in feelings, attitudes, and behavior may be lacking or minimal within a large group. (For a further study of this, see *Learning Is Change* by Martha Leypoldt and *Ways to Help Them Learn—Adults* by H. Norman Wright. It takes so much longer to bring about lasting change with large groups than with the smaller group and proper methods.

Here are two examples to illustrate this problem. A typical way in which to teach fathers and mothers their roles and responsibilities would be to bring thirty, forty, or fifty couples together for a series of training sessions. A better procedure would be to train five or ten couples for several months. At times the entire family might be together. Following their training period, these couples would become teachers and minister within groups of two or three other families.

For courses on marriage and husband-and-wife relationships, why not take eight or ten couples and meet with them for two or three hours each training session for several months. They in turn would minister to eight or ten other couples. This isn't to say that large-group sessions cannot bring results; they can. But more lasting results can be achieved with smaller groups. The instructor can give more individual attention; there is more opportunity for using methods which will affect change; and there is more opportunity for personal application and interaction with others. The principles for bringing about change can work to their fullest in this type of environment.

WHAT IS BEING DONE?

The following organizations or programs illustrate what is being done to (1) train pastors and other professionals and (2) minister to lay couples.

For the past eight years the Catholic church has operated the Marriage Encounter program, an extensive forty-four-hour weekend experience for married couples. Marriage Encounter is conducted by priests and married couples. The reports and responses to this program have been quite positive, and this pattern ought to be investigated in depth by evangelical Christians.[13]

The Christian Marriage Enrichment Seminar program was developed in 1974 for the twofold purpose of enriching the marriage relationship of pastors and their wives and equipping them to conduct similar marriage seminars in their own churches. The philosophy of this organization is that pastors and selected qualified lay couples from their own local churches are best qualified to minister to their congregation. For two days the couples (the number is limited to forty couples) work together on marriage goals, the purpose and expectations of marriage, communication, family roles and responsibilities, decision making, and conflict within marriage. These seminars are held across the United States, and at the present time between three and four hundred couples have been trained. Follow-up studies indicate that this approach has been successful, and pastors report they have waiting lists for the classes and seminars they are conducting for their own couples. For detailed information write to CMES, 13800 Biola Ave., La Mirada, California 90639.

ACME is the Association of Couples for Marriage Enrichment. This new organization was founded by Dr. and Mrs. David Mace, noted counselors and writers. Couples in this program undertake to support and help each other in seeking growth and enrichment in their own marriage; they promote and support effective community services to foster successful marriages; and they are dedicated to improve public acceptance and understanding of marriage as a relationship capable of fostering personal growth and mutual fulfillment. Through a monthly newsletter and local chapter meetings, married couples are given assistance. For complete information write to ACME, 403 S. Hawthorne Road, Winston-Salem, North Carolina 27103.

Another national organization designed to promote healthy family life through training professionals is the National Alliance for Family Life founded by Dr. James Rue. For complete information write to NAFL, 505 Fifth St., Huntington Beach, California 92648.

An example of what local churches have done should indicate that creative ventures are possible in local churches. A program entitled Neighborhood Couples' Seminars was instituted by Bethany Baptist Church in West Covina, California, for the purpose of ministering to church couples and couples referred to the church by the local police department. First, fifteen couples from the church were trained through an intensive seminar approach. Then the police department began carrying brochures describing this program. Police distributed these brochures to couples involved in a family disturbance and urged them to participate in the program. The first class met with eight police referral couples. Halfway through the course, couples previously trained by the church entered the class and participated with the referred couples. They began to invite these couples to their homes on a social basis, and through this approach many of them accepted Jesus Christ and marriages were changed. This class has been repeated on several occasions.

NOTES

1. "Report on the American Family," *Better Homes and Gardens,* 1972.

2. *National Alliance for Family Life Newsletter,* Spring 1973.

3. *Family Life Magazine,* American Institute of Family Relations, Hollywood, California, Fall 1972.

4. Alvin Toffler, *Future Shock* (New York: Random House, 1970), p. 251.

5. David Augsburger, *Cherishable: Love and Marriage* (Scottdale, Pa.: Herald Press, 1972), p. 16.

6. Carl Rogers, *Becoming Partners: Marriage and Its Alternatives* (New York: Delacorte Press, Dell Publishing Co., 1973), p. 11.

7. Richard Lessor, *Love and Marriage and Trading Stamps* (Niles, Ill.: Argus Communications, 1971), p. 7.

8. Vida Deen, "Family Conflict Calls Major Police Concern," *Santa Ana Register,* 28 March 1973.

9. William Lederer, in *Marriage For and Against,* ed. Harold H. Hart (New York: Hart, 1971), p. 137.

10. Deen, "Family Conflict Calls Major Police Concern."

11. Nathan Ackerman, in Lederer, *Marriage For and Against.*

12. Ibid.

13. For more details, see Henry Durkin, *Forty-Four Hours to Change Your Life—Marriage Encounter* (Paramus, N.J.: Paulist Press, 1974).

SUGGESTED RESOURCES

BOOKS

Jackson, Don D., and Lederer, William J. *The Mirages of Marriage.* New York: Norton, 1968.

Knox, David. *Marriage—Who? When? Why?* Englewood Cliffs, N.J.: Prentice-Hall, 1974.

Leypoldt, Martha. *Learning Is Change.* Valley Forge, Pa.: Judson Press, 1971.

Minnesota Couples Communication Program Handbook. MCCP, 2001 Riverside Ave., Minneapolis, Minnesota 55404.

Olthius, James. *I Pledge You My Troth.* New York: Harper & Row, 1975.

Osborne, Cecil. *The Art of Understanding Your Mate.* Grand Rapids, Mich.: Zondervan, 1970.

Satir, Virginia. *Conjoint Family Therapy.* Palo Alto, Cal.: Science and Behavior Books, 1967.

Wherloos, Sven. *Family Communication.* New York: Macmillan, 1974.

Wiebe, R. *Tell Me Again, I'm Listening.* Nashville, Tenn.: Abingdon, 1973.

Wright, H. Norman. *Communication—Key to Your Marriage.* Glendale, Cal.: Regal Books, 1974. This book contains a teacher-leader's guide and a class text.

————. *Ways to Help Them Learn—Adults.* Glendale, Cal.: Regal Books, 1972.

CURRICULA

The Christian Faces . . . Emotions, Marriage, and Family Life. A four-month course for married couples with additional courses for up to a year of classes. Order from CME, 1070 Detroit St., Denver, Col. $7.95.

Miller, Levi. *The Family in Today's Society*. Scottdale, Pa.: Herald Press, 1972. Contains a workbook and cassette for case studies and examples. $8.95.

FILMS

Encounter. A series of six one-minute discussion spots. Order from St. Franciscan Productions, 1229 S. Santre St., Los Angeles, Cal., or from your Christian film distributor.
Nobody Important. Excellent for discussion purposes.
Johnny Lingo. Focuses upon self-esteem within marriage.
Do You Ever Wonder? Produced by Johnson and Nyquist Productions.

TESTS AND EVALUATION FORMS

Taylor Johnson Temperament Analysis. A personality test that has been used for teaching and evaluation. See *The Christian Faces* (listed under Curricula) for complete information on training to use this test and biblical application.
The Marital Communication Inventory and *The Marriage Expectation Inventory for Married Couples*. Family Life Publications, Box 427, Saluda, N.C. 28773. Costs less than 20 cents per copy.
The Marital Pre-Counseling Inventory. Research Press, 2612 N. Mattis, Champaign, Ill. 61820. Assists couples in evaluating their marriage.

CASSETTES

Christenson, Larry. *The Christian Husband; The Christian Wife*. Bethany Fellowship, Minneapolis, Minn.
Seamands, David. *Love, Honor, and Forgive; Looking at Our Goals in Marriage; Factors That Make Up a Christian Marriage*. Order from Tape Ministries, Box 3389, Pasadena, Cal. 91103.
Sproul, R. C. *Sex in Marriage*. Thompson Media, Stahlstown, Pa. 15687.
Wright, Norman. *Communication—Key to Your Marriage*. Order from CME, 1070 Detroit St., Denver, Col.
Wheat, Ed. *Sex Problems and Sex Techniques in Marriage*. Order from CME, 1070 Detroit St., Denver, Col.

12

A Christian Perspective on Alternative Styles of Marriage

JOHN SCANZONI

In thinking about Alternative Styles of Marriage (ASM), at least three questions confront us immediately. First, these styles are alternatives to what? Second, why would persons seek these alternatives? Finally, is the search for ASM a recent innovation or does it have a longer history?

Taking the historical question first, it is clear that ASM is not a new notion. Going back to nineteenth-century America, we find several communal experiments with variations in family forms.[1] Some of these existed in a Christian context such as the Shakers who espoused celibacy. Going back hundreds of years, there is the Roman Catholic tradition of some women remaining celibate, "marrying Christ," and living in community.

Therefore, if the notion of ASM is not new, why have they emerged in the past or in the present? It must be that some persons feel that prevailing family life styles were or are not adequate to meet their own interests. In the cases of Catholic nuns and of Shakers, there are religious interests which cannot be met through Traditional Family Forms (TFF). Therefore they created new

JOHN SCANZONI is professor of sociology at Indiana University, where he has taught since 1964. He is the author of six books, including *Men, Women, and Change: A Sociology of Marriage and Family,* which he coauthored with his wife Letha, and *Sex Roles, Life-Styles and Childbearing.* He has also written many journal and magazine articles, and travels widely speaking on marriage and the family. The Scanzonis have two sons.

forms to meet those religious interests. And so it is today. Some persons feel that TFF are simply inadequate to allow them to achieve what they consider to be significant and overriding interests. Consequently, they experiment with ASM.

and that leads to our first question—what is TFF? What are the dominant and prevailing forms which an increasing minority of persons find inadequate for their own interests? Stated briefly, the great majority of families in the United States and in all industrialized societies are organized in terms of one male and one female legally married and having borne at least one child, usually more. If they haven't had children, they intend to get some—either through their own physiological efforts or by adoption. The husband is considered the chief provider for the family, and because of that the family's station in life as well as its major activities center around him. His job, for example, determines where the family shall live. In addition, his provider role gives him considerable authority in the household over the lives and destinies of his wife and children. And though an increasing number of wives are working, in most instances such jobs are secondary to the husband's job (or career) in their significance for the family's long- and short-term social and economic well-being.

Precisely that pattern is being scrutinized, criticized, and minimized. There are at least ten different ASM which in one way or another modify TFF. We shall briefly discuss all ten, evaluate each one in Christian perspective, and suggest which of these promise to be permanent innovations and not merely limited fads.[2]

TRIAL MARRIAGE

In this ASM, a man and woman live together without a license. They have sexual access to each other, but obviously they do not want any pregnancies. They do want to find out if they are "suited" for each other. Can they learn to negotiate and strike bargains that each will find profitable? If so, they would marry; if not, they would cease living together. They want to avoid what they consider the blandness or else intolerableness of many marriages among persons over thirty. They also want to avoid the acrimony and economic costs of legal divorce decrees. However, persons favoring this ASM tend to overlook the fact that no matter what bargain a couple strikes at marriage—whether there has been trial or not—*change* inevitably occurs. If one's long-term goal is the most satisfying marriage possible, a trial run at the outset is not the whole of it. In any case, some persons have proposed that states legalize the notion of a trial period—a license for cohabitation but not parenthood. If that period proves satisfactory, decisions regarding a permanent license (and the parenthood option) could be made.

The fundamental premise of trial marriage is that persons should *think,* should be rational, *before* entering legal marriage. The myth of romantic love overwhelming persons and sweeping them unthinkingly to the altar is exposed for what it is—a fiction that does enormous harm, especially to persons who can afford it least—those with less education. Significantly, the emphasis on rationality regarding marriage decisions is a biblical principle enunciated in Matthew 19 and 1 Corinthians 7. However, while Christians can endorse premarital rationality, the question of premarital sex is something else. Many Christians believe that coitus prior to marriage is not God's will for Christians.[3] Others might take a more permissive view and allow it under certain conditions, for example, engaged couples close to marriage.

It is likely that among non-Christians in the future an increasing number will opt for trial arrangements, perhaps several over time, each with a different partner. Eventually, however, most will enter a legal union. Among Christians we may expect greater emphasis on prayerful rationality regarding marriage decisions but continued hesitancy to engage in coitus prior to actual marriage. That raises a fundamental question posed by many persons today—what constitutes a marriage? There is considerable distaste and disdain for the notion that a license per se makes a marriage. Some argue that "love" and sharing together make a marriage and that a license is irrelevant. Indeed, one may point to the Isaac and Rebekah narrative to show that licensing is not a biblical notion (Gen. 24). But throughout the Bible and indeed throughout the social science literature it is clear that there is no such thing as "private marriage" —one shared only by the two persons involved.[4] Marriage is public, and if two persons declare that they now share economic and sexual interdependences, and their community or society does nothing to subvert their union, they are married in the social sense. For example, in 1877 the United States Supreme Court established the principle which holds today that "common-law marriages are valid unless the state in question has a specific law which declares them to be illegal."[5] (Currently, more than two-thirds of the states prohibit common-law or "social" marriage.) Unfortunately space does not permit us to dwell on the complex implications of a purely "social" marriage.[6] However for reasons too lengthy to be detailed here, it would seem that Christians, while recognizing the fundamental reality of their social union and their mutual troth before God, would want to go the "second mile," not give "unnecessary offense" (1 Cor. 10:32), and go ahead and obtain the license even though they may recognize its "spiritual irrelevance."

AD HOC ARRANGEMENTS

The main feature that distinguishes the ad hoc arrangements pattern from trial marriage is that persons do not define their partner as a potential licensed mate. They are simply "shacking up" and shall continue to do so until they "split."

SINGLENESS

In recent years census data show a steady increase in the proportion of younger men and women who never marry legally.[7] Moreover, reversing the downward trend of many decades, the median age at first marriage is rising. Those who marry are now doing so at a later age, thus staying single longer. The greatest thrust for singleness as an ASM comes from the feminist movement. Younger women (and some men) seriously question whether marriage is necessarily more desirable than singleness, as most people (including Christians) in modern societies seem to believe. For most women marriage has meant giving up autonomy, freedom, and self-direction. It has often meant giving up opportunities to use one's own unique gifts and talents in service to God, church, and society. Her talents and interests have most often become subordinated to his. Therefore in order to maintain autonomy, and sometimes integrity, increasing numbers of younger women (and some men) are concluding that singleness is more desirable than marriage, or at least as viable an option.

Christians can have no quarrel with that because the New

Testament makes it clear that singleness is indeed as viable an option as marriage. If anything, both Christ and Paul indicate that the most dedicated saints remain single so that they can serve God in ways that family responsibilities would prevent. That conviction has been the basis of Catholic celibacy for hundreds of years.

SINGLE PARENTHOOD

Most persons are forced into becoming solo parents either because of the death of their spouse or because of divorce. Most of these persons would prefer to remarry so that the burdens of parenthood can be shared. But for some persons an emerging ASM is one in which they enjoy the rewards of parenthood but prefer to avoid the costs of marriage. As more and more states permit adoption by a single person, this becomes one route to single parenthood. There is the Catholic priest, for example, who actually has four legally adopted children. And while the single woman who becomes pregnant has recourse to legal abortion or to giving up her newborn, a certain number are purposely choosing to keep their infants—choosing in effect to become "single parents."[8] Other women who prefer single parenthood may seek pregnancy through artificial insemination.

Currently however we know from census that most solo parent households are female-headed and that most are poor with numerous children present. Studies indicate that most of these women would prefer a husband.[9] In such situations children suffer, not because one parent is absent, but because of the poverty.[10] However, children are not likely to suffer in situations where a capable, well-educated person purposely chooses, for instance, to adopt merely one or two. Therefore, in the future we may expect that among those persons who prefer singleness as a life style, some will nevertheless opt for parenthood.

CHILD-FREE MARRIAGE

In contrast to persons who want to avoid marriage but experience parenthood, there is an increasing minority of younger persons who are legally married but who definitely want to avoid the costs of parenthood. The terms *voluntary childlessness* or *child-free* marriage characterize this ASM. In the past it was assumed that if one married one automatically eventually made the transition to parenthood. Not wanting as many children as one could reasonably care for was considered selfish, irresponsible, immature—less than adult.[11] In 1967 the Census Bureau found that among younger (18–24) married women without children, only 1 percent expected *never* to have any children. But by 1974, that figure had risen to 5 percent, and among women with some college the figure was close to 10 percent.[12]

During this same interval NON was formed (the National Organization of Non-Parents). Worries about overpopulation, pollution, and food and energy shortages made large families less moral and defensible than they once were. It also became abundantly clear that not all adults made good parents; some were terrible at the task. Moreover, it became plain how financially costly children are and how difficult it is to get along with them—especially during the adolescent and young adult periods. Added to all of these is the emergence of the dual-career marriage—a phenomenon we shall examine in detail below. When wives are just as active as husbands at occupational achievement, child-care issues can cause considerable conflict. They can also complicate geographic mobility for either or both achievers, as well as complicate leisure activities for persons who prefer other than the usual "family-type" vacations.

Therefore, while the overwhelming majority of couples still plan to have at least one child, there are those who opt for none. There is nothing in the New Testament to suggest that Christian couples must have children. Recently, some Christians have raised the possibility that we ought to consider childless marriages as a "vocation" or "special calling" which frees certain couples to perform ministries that otherwise would not be possible.[13] Christian couples who opt to be childless should do so in prayerful and careful fashion, consulting other Christians and seeking out a variety of viewpoints on the matter. By the same reasoning they should be just as prayerful before they decide to become parents. Why not say to a trusted Christian friend: "Level with me and honestly tell me whether you think I would make a good parent?" It is obviously much simpler for a child-free than for a parenting couple to change their life style.

COMMUNAL LIVING

There are so many varieties of this type of ASM that we could not possibly do justice to all of them in this short space.[14] We noted earlier that communal living has been part of Christian experience for a long time. Today there has been a renewal of emphasis on community among Christians.[15] Some Christians believe that living in community is a way to lower their economic life style and to utilize excess capital assets to benefit the less-advantaged. The most successful communes anywhere in the world are the Israeli kibbutzim. In most communes there is no private ownership of capital or of major goods. While there is economic sharing including sharing of households, in only a few is there anything like sexual sharing. In most instances, and certainly in Christian communes (for example, the "Jesus People"),[16] the sexually monogamous marriage is preferred. However emotional ties and decision making for the couple lie with the entire community, not merely between husband and wife. Along with economic sharing those are the two features that distinguish most communities from the traditional conjugal family.

Clearly, many Christians have come to find community much more viable than traditional family forms. In the future we may expect this phenomenon to continue to remain part of Christian experience, with perhaps a gradual increase in its incidence. A variation on community which will probably attract even greater numbers is the "intimate network."[17] In this situation married couples maintain separate households and ultimate control of their own material assets, but emotional and financial help along with pragmatic services are fully shared among participating couples according to their particular abilities and needs.

GROUP MARRIAGE

This ASM involves three or more usually heterosexual persons who share both economically and sexually. Any children born are considered to belong to the whole group. All persons in the group (common household) consider themselves married to all other persons, though of course legally the limit is one. These kinds of arrangements tend to be much smaller than commune-type groups and even more unstable. There is considerable turnover of persons in and out of group marriages; and the arrangements themselves are quite prone to total dissolution.

MATE SWAPPING

Also known as "swinging" or "group sex," this ASM may be characterized as extramarital sex for both partners by mutual consent within a highly structured set of rules and regulations.[18] Swingers' networks and magazines enable interested couples to learn about swingers' clubs in their locale. There is no economic or household sharing within this ASM; decision making is not relinquished by the couple, nor are significant emotional support or pragmatic services performed. Moreover the behavior is covert in that the couple does not tell children, relatives, and "straight" friends about their swinging. Sex is shared, however, in a context in which wives participate jointly with their husbands—in contrast to the past where it was mostly men who engaged in "cheating" or covert adultery. It must be emphasized that swinging sessions are not free-for-all orgies but highly routinized patterns of heterosexual (and less often lesbian and homosexual) behaviors among married couples. (Singles are usually not welcome.) Generally the stated purpose of swinging is to "spice up" married sex that has become afflicted with "sameness." Needless to say, most Christians would agree that either group marriage or mate swapping would put them in violation of the commandment on adultery.

GAY MARRIAGE

In contrast to promiscuous homosexuality, a gay marriage (the legality of which is uncertain) involves a long-term commitment by two persons of the same sex to each other. They do not seek sex outside their relationship. Some Christians defend these arrangements, and there is a national network of community churches which provide social support for persons in gay marriages.[19] In addition, gays seek legitimation of their marriages from established mainline churches such as the UPUSA or the United Methodist Church.

DUAL-CAREER MARRIAGE

What emerging ASM will be the most permanent? Which is not merely faddish? Which will be around many years into the future? Which will most profoundly change the structure of marriage away from forms that now prevail? The TFF described earlier in which the husband is chief provider and therefore ultimate authority? Almost all serious researchers concur that Western marriage has been evolving in a certain direction for at least one hundred fifty years and that inexorably, though gradually, it will continue to move in that direction. One group of English social scientists describes that evolution as a movement toward the *symmetrical* family.[20] A second group of English investigators calls it the *dual-career* or *dual-achiever* pattern.[21] In the United States it has been labeled the *co-provider marriage,* or one in which major marital roles are interchangeable rather than specialized according to sex.[22]

In modern societies the most highly valued and rewarded activities occur in the world of work. These rewards are not merely material, but equally if not more important, they are intangible as well: identity, respect, dignity, status, meaning, prestige, honor, worthiness. In the past, the married woman worked chiefly for material rewards, to "help out" the family. Rarely did she seek the same sorts of intangible gratifications as her husband. He had the *right* to gain those rewards and the *responsibility* to provide for his wife. She had the *responsibility* to take care of the household and the *right* to expect support. *It is precisely that neat order of things that is evaporating.* Younger, well-educated women want the right to the intangible and tangible rewards of occupational achievement, and none can reasonably say them nay. Yea, simple justice and complex federal law demand it. With those rights comes a shift in her responsibilities—she must now provide for her family but she no longer is chiefly responsible for the household. Obviously there must likewise come a corresponding shift in the husband's rights and duties: he now *shares* with his wife the right to achieve; he *gains* the right to be provided for; he *shares* his duties to provide; and picks up duties to help care for the household.[23]

The notion that work or vocation is a sacred calling from God permeates the whole Bible, and nowhere, it seems to me, can defensible grounds be found to deny any vocations to married women—including ordination.[24] It therefore follows that women should be free to pursue their vocations as diligently as do men, in other words to seek to achieve to the fullest extent of their God-given gifts. The best biblical model of this "emerging" ASM is Priscilla and Aquila.

In short, over the next several decades at least, we may expect monogamous legal marriage to be the predominant pattern that most persons in modern and emerging societies will choose. However for a steadily increasing percentage of couples, its structure will undergo basic change in that women by virtue of their occupational endeavors will become co-providers with men. Therefore processes within marriage will change, the most fundamental of which is that of authority. Women both in and out of marriage will increasingly become the *genuine* equals of men. Genuine equality plainly means that there is no "fixed" or ultimate head; power is shared equally. Justice and affirmation become more crucial than who has the "final say."

Christians can welcome this emergence because it is a thoroughly biblical alternative.[25] This emerging form is not utopian; it will not solve all problems. No human arrangement is perfect because of selfishness and greed. No arrangement—whether traditional or emerging—is without its unique pains and sufferings. But clearly, currently prevailing forms (TFF) are unsatisfactory for many reasons, not least of which is that they permit men to be selfish (often unconsciously), women to be exploited (often by default), and church and society to be deprived of the gifts God has given to women. This emerging ASM will help to correct those ills. For that reason alone, and for others too numerous to mention here, it seems to me that Christians ought to respond positively to the difficulties and opportunities it brings. To do otherwise will mean we have learned nothing from the mistakes of our *fathers* in other areas (for example, political, racial, economic discrimination) and to misread both "the signs of the times" and the Scriptures.

NOTES

1. Letha Scanzoni and John Scanzoni, *Men, Women, and Change: A Sociology of Marriage and Family* (New York: McGraw-Hill, 1976).

2. More thorough discussions are found in John Scanzoni, *Sexual Bargaining: Power Politics in American Marriage* (Englewood Cliffs, N.J.: Prentice-Hall, 1972); Letha Scanzoni, *Why Wait? A Christian View of Premarital Sex* (Grand Rapids, Mich.: Baker Book House, 1975); and Scanzoni and Scanzoni, *Men, Women, and Change*.

3. Letha Scanzoni, *Why Wait?*

4. James Olthius, *I Pledge You My Troth* (New York: Harper & Row, 1975).

5. William Kephart, "Legal and Procedural Aspects of Marriage and Divorce," in Harold T. Christensen, ed., *Handbook of Marriage and the Family* (Chicago: Rand McNally, 1964), pp. 944–68.

6. For further elaborations see Scanzoni and Scanzoni, *Men, Women, and Change*, and John Scanzoni, *Sexual Bargaining*.

7. Scanzoni and Scanzoni, *Men, Women, and Change*.

8. Lisa Connolly, "Little Mothers," *Human Behavior* 4:16–23.

9. Lee Rainwater, *Family Design: Marital Sexuality, Family Size, and Contraception* (Chicago: Aldine, 1965).

10. P. M. Blau and O. D. Duncan, *The American Occupational Structure* (New York: Wiley, 1967).

11. Rainwater, *Family Design*.

12. Scanzoni and Scanzoni, *Men, Women, and Change*.

13. J. H. Yoder, "Singleness and Pastoral Perspective," Mennonite Biblical Seminaries, Elkhart, Ind., 1975; William and Julie Everett, "Childless Marriages: A New Vocation?" *U.S. Catholic*, May 1975, pp. 38–39.

14. See Scanzoni and Scanzoni, *Men, Women, and Change*.

15. See Dave and Neta Jackson, *Living Together in a World Falling Apart* (Carol Stream, Ill.: Creation House, 1974).

16. Jack Balswick, "The Jesus People Movement: A Sociological Analysis," in P. H. McNamara, ed., *Religion American Style* (New York: Harper & Row, 1974).

17. John Scanzoni, *Sexual Bargaining*.

18. Scanzoni and Scanzoni, *Men, Women, and Change*.

19. Ronald M. Enroth and Gerald E. Jamison, *The Gay Church* (Grand Rapids, Mich.: Eerdmans, 1973).

20. M. Young and P. Willmott, *The Symmetrical Family* (London: Routledge & Kegan Paul, 1973).

21. Michael P. Fogarty, Rhona Rapoport, and Robert N. Rapoport, *Sex, Career, and Family* (Beverly Hills: Sage, 1971).

22. Lynda Lytle Holmstrom, *The Two-Career Family* (Cambridge, Mass.: Schenkman, 1972); John Scanzoni, *Sexual Bargaining*.

23. For a fuller elaboration of these shifts in rights and duties, see John Scanzoni, *Sexual Bargaining*.

24. John Scanzoni, "The Christian View of Work," in C. F. H. Henry, ed., *Quest for Reality: Christianity and the Counter Culture* (Downers Grove, Ill.: Inter-Varsity Press, 1973).

25. Letha Scanzoni and Nancy Hardesty, *All We're Meant to Be: A Biblical Approach to Women's Liberation* (Waco, Tex.: Word Books, 1974); John Scanzoni, "Authority in Christian Marriage," *Reformed Journal* 24:2–24.

Study Guide

GARY R. COLLINS

The purpose of a study guide is to help individuals or groups of readers better understand, evaluate and interact with the ideas that are presented in a book or collection of articles. The chapters which comprise the preceding pages contain a number of insights and sometimes conflicting opinions, and are written by capable people who have given serious thought to marriage as it exists and is changing today. By adding a study guide to this book, it is hoped that you will be encouraged and helped to think back over what has been written and to arrive at some further conclusions of your own.

It is possible, of course, to work through this study guide on your own or with your spouse, but you might find group discussion to be more beneficial and interesting. The study guide has been designed, therefore, for individual study which leads to group interaction. Whenever a group meets, there should be a leader (or a couple) who can guide the discussion and stimulate interaction. The same leader(s) can direct all of the discussions, or you may want to shift leadership responsibilities so that a different person or couple, chosen from the group, leads each session.

Before meeting, each group member should read the chapter or chapters to be discussed and look over the questions which follow. These questions are designed to stimulate discussion and at times may lead to lively debate. The leader(s) should encourage everyone to express his or her views, should maintain a somewhat objective perspective in the group, and should try to keep the discussion from getting too far off the track. When there are irreconcilable differences, the leader(s) should have the right to stop discussion until more homework can be done, expert advice can be obtained, or the group agrees that discussion has reached a dead end.

The last question or two in each section focuses on the church's role in ministering to the married. You might wish to discuss these questions in your group even if you are not a church leader. If you do so, try to come up with constructive (rather than destructive) criticisms of your church's present programs, and be specific in your suggestions for future changes.

One final comment: the questions and exercises which follow are merely suggestive. If you can think of questions which are better, more controversial or of greater benefit to you and your group, use them. It might be more fun that way!

Chapter 1: Lloyd Ogilvie
Marriage As It Was Meant to Be

PREPARATION

1. Lloyd Ogilvie's chapter is both a call for churches to become more involved in building better marriages, and a challenge for married people to think about their own marriages. As you read the chapter, ask yourself, "How can *my* church be involved in building better marriages?" and "What can *I* do to improve my own marriage?" Jot down your answers and discuss them with your spouse.

2. Turn in your Bible to Mark 10:1–12 and carefully read the passage that Ogilvie discusses in his chapter.

MEETING TOGETHER

3. To get started, the group members (including the leader) should introduce themselves. Indicate why you are in the discussion group. What do you hope the group will accomplish?

4. If this has not been clarified previously, decide how often the group will meet, for what length of time, what chapter or chapters will be discussed at each meeting, and how the leadership responsibilities will be handled. Will the same individual or couple always lead or will leadership responsibilities rotate between group members?

5. Ogilvie makes a number of challenging statements in his chapter. Consider the following, for example. Do you agree, partially agree, or disagree with each? Give reasons for your answers.

a. "Our frenzied quest for marriage as the alternative to frustration and unfulfillment is inconsistent with God's plan. . . . Marriage is not the answer to the dilemma of life or loneliness!"

b. "Unless we love God more than our mate, we can never love our mate, really!"

c. "A marriage is most Christian, not when it is free of problems and difficulties, but when two persons open themselves to the Spirit of Christ, surrender their wills to him, commit their living to him, and as a conscious dedication, seek to love each other and give themselves to each other as they have been loved and given to by Christ."

d. "Christian honesty is not telling another person his faults; it is being honest before God about ourselves and our failures."

e. "Most frustrations in marriage come from unexpressed desires and uncommunicated dreams."

6. Ogilvie states that we should not "wring our hands at the divorce statistics, but uncover the essential nature of marriage as God intended it to be." Based on your reading of this chapter and your study of the Bible, what is the "essential nature of marriage as God intended it to be"?

7. The chapter identifies five "building blocks" to better marriage: honesty, vulnerability, working contracts, initiative love, and affirmation. What do each of these terms mean? In what specific ways can they be developed to improve marriages in your church? How can these be used in your life to improve your own marriage?

8. Even the best marriage has room for improvement. What do you think of Ogilvies "thirty-day experiment"? Would it work in your marriage? Why not try it and in one month report to the group how it worked?

QUESTIONS FOR CHURCH LEADERS

9. What is the state of your marriage? Is it "open and vulnerable" enough to be seen by the congregation as a "frontier of your growing faith"? If not, how can your marriage be improved? How could your church hold the kind of marriage enrichment conference described by Ogilvie? Discuss these questions with the church leadership.

Chapter 2: Louis and Colleen Evans
Gifts of the Spirit in Marriage

PREPARATION

1. Louis and Colleen Evans propose a controversial and thought-provoking idea in this chapter—that the relationship between a husband and wife should be based more on the gifts and abilities which each possesses and less on the traditional roles which a husband and wife are supposed to fill. What do you think about this idea? Make a list of your gifts and list the gifts of your spouse.

2. The Bible discusses spiritual gifts in Romans 12, 1 Corinthians 12 and Ephesians 4. Turn to 1 Corinthians 12 and read the whole chapter. Does this cause you to alter the lists that you made in response to question 1 above?

MEETING TOGETHER

3. In the first half of their chapter, the Evans propose three theses. What are these theses? Do you agree, partially agree, or disagree with the authors' conclusions? Discuss the theses one at a time and give reasons for your opinions.

4. How do you respond to the following quotations?

a. "The Holy Spirit gives to each spouse some gift or gifts . . . for the functioning of the home. . . . Therefore, each home should be sensitive to the gifts of each person. . . . This is true for spouses and children alike."

b. A woman "is 'helper' to man, yes, but that does not imply inferiority. . . . Some roles are determined by sex, but most are determined by the gifts of the Spirit."

c. Some speakers "ask Christian women to do the wrong a husband requires, in order to carry out their submission to him. . . . We have seen more women win their husbands by standing up for their faith and its responsibilities, and speaking the truth in love, than those who denied the expression of their faith in hopes of bringing him around."

5. The authors imply that the Apostle Paul "put women down" in his writing. Do you think that the Bible treats women as second-class people? Give reasons for your answer. What has this got to do with marriage?

6. The authors identify two extreme views with which they disagree. The one shouts "down with motherhood," the other shouts "women, submit to your husbands in everything." Do you agree that these are extreme views? What is good or bad about each of them?

7. How would your marriage be different if you and your spouse tried to forget traditional husband-wife roles and built a marriage based on each other's gifts? Would such a relationship be biblical?

QUESTIONS FOR CHURCH LEADERS

8. What is taught in your church about the role and duties of the husband and wife? What does the Bible teach? In view of the Evanses' chapter, do you think there should be a change in what your church teaches? Ponder these questions as you read the next two chapters.

Chapter 3: Larry Christenson
A New Look at Christian Husbands

PREPARATION

1. How can a man be a good husband at a time when marriages are falling apart and some women's groups are demanding more "rights" for wives? After reading Larry Christenson's chapter ask yourself, "What are the characteristics of a good husband?" If you are married, discuss this with your spouse.

2. Turn to a modern translation of the Bible and read Ephesians 5:21–33, the passage Christenson discusses in his chapter. What does this Scripture teach *you* about the responsibilities of husbands?

MEETING TOGETHER

3. Begin your group discussion by sharing your reaction to the following quotations taken from the chapter. In each case try to answer these questions: "Do I agree, partly agree or disagree? What are the reasons for my answer? In what practical ways does this quotation help to improve husbands?"

a. "You can't be a man as far as God is concerned unless you are under the headship of Christ."

b. "A wife is meant to live behind the protective shield of her husband in relationships outward to the community and also within the family."

c. "To love with no ties, no commitment . . . is the most conservative, selfish kind of love one could imagine! It wants to give nothing. It will not risk a single thing. The most daring kind of love commits itself totally to marriage."

d. "Satan hates sex because he sees that it is something God created as a great gift for man and woman to enjoy within the circle of marriage. That is why he does everything he can to get that gift operating outside the confines of marriage. . . ."

4. In his discussion of Ephesians 5, Christenson identifies five roles for the husband. What is the first of these? What are some specific ways in which a husband can show his wife that he loves her? Why don't husbands more often show their love in these ways? Will this change in your marriage?

5. What is *agapē* love? How does the example of Hosea show this kind of love? How can husbands (and wives) in your discussion group show *agapē* love?

6. Christenson maintains that the "husband as sanctifier" is responsible to help his wife become (a) holy and (b) "wholly the Lord's." Do you agree that this is the husband's responsibility? How can a husband help his wife in these two areas? What can she do to help herself?

7. What is your opinion about working wives? Do you agree with Christenson that whether or not the wife works, "the fundamental responsibility in providing for the family still rests upon the husband"?

8. Christenson suggests that the average family has "too many captains." All members of the family are "trying to run the ship in their own power and authority." Do you agree with this analysis? Give reasons for your answer. How can the family ship be better run? Is your answer consistent with the Bible's teaching? In what practical ways could your family ship be run better? When are you going to bring about these changes?

QUESTIONS FOR CHURCH LEADERS

9. What is your church doing to help men become better husbands? Are you helping young single men in the church to prepare for marriage? Think of some practical and specific ways to help men become better husbands. How could your suggestions be put into effect?

Chapter 4: Gladys Hunt
A New Look at Christian Wives

PREPARATION

1. After reading the chapter by Gladys Hunt, ask yourselves a question about wives similar to the question asked about husbands in the

previous chapter: "What are the characteristics of a good wife?" If you are married, discuss this with your spouse.

2. One of the most beautiful and thought-provoking statements about wives is found in Proverbs 31. Read verses 10–31. What implications, if any, does this chapter have for modern marriages? What are the implications for your marriage?

MEETING TOGETHER

3. In her chapter, Hunt mentions the thinking about wives held by Letha Scanzoni and Nancy Hardesty (authors of *All We're Meant To Be*), Marabel Morgan (*The Total Woman*), and Bill Gothard. Are there members in your group who can summarize the viewpoints of these people? Why does Hunt resist these and other popular views of what it means to be a wife? Do you agree with Hunt? Why?

4. This chapter gives a "new call to Christian wives to maintain, to insist upon, to establish quality relationships" with their husbands. How can this be done? Hunt suggests the following:

"be open with each other, sharing deeply, transparent in the most intimate areas of life, forgiving each other, serving each other, transcending self to enhance and affirm each other."

Can you state this formula in more practical terms? How could it work to build better husband-wife relationships? Would it work in your marriage?

5. This chapter makes several references to the biblical command for wives to be in submission to their husbands. Someone in the group might read Ephesians 5:22–24 and 1 Peter 3:1; then discuss in practical terms what it means for a wife to be submissive to her husband. Do you agree that some wives pretend to submit but in so doing really manipulate their husbands? According to the Bible, how should the Christian wife relate to her husband? Is the husband-wife relationship to be different if the Christian wife has a nonbelieving husband?

6. Hunt stresses the importance of a wife (and husband) having a high view of self. Is it OK for Christians to think well of themselves, or should we view ourselves as worthless? Give reasons for your answer. What has this got to do with marriage?

7. Sometimes it is stated by Christians that when a husband and wife "become one," they lose their personality in each other. In this chapter, however, the author maintains that "nothing is more misleading than a view of oneness that reduces two people to an amalgamated blob, in which both persons lose their identity. A blob cannot relate." How can two persons (like you and your spouse) become one without losing their separate identities?

8. What is your church doing to help women become better wives? Are you helping young single women in the church to prepare for marriage? Think of some practical and specific ways to help women become better wives. How could your suggestions be put into effect?

Chapter 5: Mark W. Lee
Reasons Marriages Fail: Communication

PREPARATION

1. A failure to communicate is at the basis of many marriage problems. In this chapter Mark Lee helps us to understand how communication can be improved, not only in marriage, but in our families and elsewhere. As you read the chapter keep asking yourself, "What does this say that would help me to communicate better?" Try to apply the author's suggestions to your own marriage.

2. The Bible makes a number of statements about communication. Look, for example, at the following and think how each should have a bearing on your manner of communication: Psalm 5:8, 9; Proverbs 12:18, 19, 22; 15:1–4; James 3:5–10.

MEETING TOGETHER

3. In the first half of his paper, Lee lists what he calls " 'the dirty dozen' in verbal communication problems"—twelve types of words that can create problems in the home. As a group, try to think of some examples of each of these twelve kinds of words. Which ones do you use most frequently? Are you willing to change? Can spouses help each other to change? How?

4. What is your reaction to the following suggestions by Lee?

a. "Avoid the use of words like *always* or *never*. A helpful motto is: 'Never use never.' "

b. "Listening is vital to effective communication, and listeners take too little responsibility for their part in the communication cycle." "Without a willingness to listen intently to one another, members of any family will tend not to communicate very well with each other."

c. "Seldom does a person mean to deliberately offend another. . . . Most persons are offended by their own imaginations. They read in meanings which were unknown to the sender. They distort and twist words and attitudes."

5. Lee implies that we could communicate better if we tried to place ourselves in the position of the other person, to "live in his skin," or to see things from his point of view. Do you agree with this suggestion? What would happen if, during a disagreement, you tried to see the situation from your spouse's point of view? Would communication and/or understanding be improved?

6. The chapter says a great deal about nonverbal communication. How do people communicate apart from the use of meaningful words? How do *you* communicate nonverbally? Sometimes psychologists talk of a "double-message" in which your words say one thing but your actions say something different. Can you think of examples? What can you do to change those nonverbal communications which are harmful?

7. Our North American society encourages us not to touch other people. What are the dangers and values in touching? Do you agree that "a man or woman having been reared without physical contact may expect significant discord in marriage"? In what ways does this discussion of communication through touch influence you?

8. Lee suggests that the place where communication occurs is very important. In what ways does the environment effect communication? Does the place of meeting influence your discussion group? Does environment influence communication in your marriage?

QUESTIONS FOR CHURCH LEADERS

9. According to this chapter, one's choice of words, how words are said, and the environment all influence communication in families. Can this information be used to bring better communication within the families in your church? Can Lee's suggestions bring better communication between church members? In what specific ways could your church help members of the congregation to communicate more effectively? Is this a worthy goal for a church?

Chapter 6: Dwight H. Small
Divorce and Remarriage:
A Fresh Biblical Perspective

PREPARATION

1. In his chapter, Dwight Small deals with the Bible's teaching on divorce. This is an issue which should be of concern to all Christians, but

especially to those who are married or divorced. What is your view of divorce and remarriage? Does it correspond with one of the three positions described in the second paragraph of this chapter?

2. Divorce is discussed in several biblical passages. Read Deuteronomy 24:1–4, Matthew 19:3–12 and 1 Corinthians 7:10–16. These are the major passages which Small discusses in his chapter.

MEETING TOGETHER

3. What is your reaction to the following statements taken from Small's chapter?

a. Jesus pointed "to God's original purpose of indissoluble marriage and confirmed the continuation of that purpose. . . . There is a world of difference between allowing divorce and remarriage as an extreme solution to inescapable failure, and treating divorce and remarriage on the other hand as though they were acceptable options."

b. "Paul affirms that in general Christians are not to divorce, not that they could not, but should not."

c. "Marriage . . . is not a missionary institution! There's no guarantee that formal retention of an impossible marriage will eventually lead to the salvation of the recalcitrant partner. Don't count on that."

d. "As marital dissolution always displays human failure at best, sin at worst, may not a Christian remarriage display redemptive, renewing grace? May not God be glorified in a new marriage where mutual love and commitment, and desire for his will enable a couple to fulfill a truly 'one flesh' enduring marriage?"

e. "On God's scale of relative values for his people . . . indissoluble marriage stands high, for it alone conforms to his original intent. But personal peace is also high—higher in fact than any mere retention of a marriage which at heart is not a loving union of total persons, but a semblance only, a fraud."

4. Are divorce and remarriage sin? Always? Sometimes? Never? How do you respond to Small's statement that divorce and remarriage are never "mentioned in the listings of sins catalogued in the Epistles"? What is your reaction to the view that "in some cases, divorce and remarriage may rightfully be utilized in the service of the higher good— spiritual, emotional, personal peace without which no Christian can experience normal well-being"?

5. A major point of Small's chapter is that divorce and remarriage, while never desirable or willed by God, sometimes occur because human beings are imperfect. As Christians, therefore, we should forgive the divorced and show compassion towards them. Do you agree? Is there

ever reason for Christians to judge and withhold compassion? See Matthew 7:1.

6. According to Scripture, are divorced persons permitted to take leadership positions in the church? Read Titus 1:6 and 1 Timothy 3:2. Do you agree with Small that it "does not say 'one who has been married only once,' but clearly 'the husband of one wife.' Literally, a remarried man indeed fulfills this requirement."

7. Small maintains that a pastor should never suggest divorce regardless of how hopeless the situation. Do you agree? What would you do if your marriage was falling apart? What are you doing now to keep it from falling apart? Be specific.

QUESTIONS FOR CHURCH LEADERS

8. What and how does your church teach about divorce and remarriage? Does the pastor know what he thinks about these issues and why? What about the people in the congregation? How can the church show more compassion toward divorced persons without appearing to approve of divorce?

Chapter 7: Lars I. Granberg
Divorce and Remarriage:
Practical Implications for the Church

PREPARATION

1. What are your attitudes towards divorced people? Are you guilty of the criticism and ostracism that Lars Granberg describes in his chapter? As you read, think of divorced persons you know and ponder how your relationship with them could be more Christian and less condemning.

2. In John 4:5–29 we read about a lengthy discussion which Jesus had with a divorced woman. How was she treated? Is this surprising in view of Matthew 19:8–9? Does Jesus' example have any implications for our dealings with divorced persons today?

MEETING TOGETHER

3. According to the author of this chapter, "married couples can learn much which can strengthen their own marriage from the experience of those whose marriage has failed." What can a married

couple learn from divorced people? How can this help your own marriage?

4. Divorced people frequently are treated like "second-class members" of the church. Granberg gives three reasons for this. What are the three reasons? Is Granberg's analysis right? What about you—are you guilty of any or all three of these attitudes? How can you change?

5. Divorced people, and married people as well, often get a lot of advice on how to raise their children. According to Granberg, "the worst thing about this advice is that it tends to undercut a person's confidence in his or her own judgment as to what is and what isn't good for children." Do you agree? Can advice-giving be harmful? What about the advice that married people might give to those who are divorced or separated?

6. Discuss the following quotation from Granberg's chapter: "The Bible teaches that marriage is a covenant with the larger . . . community. Marriage is never 'nobody's business but my own.' Members of the body of Christ are to be concerned for and accountable to one another. The church in turn has a right to expect her members to offer one another acceptance and forgiveness and to be faithful to their marriage covenant."

7. In his chapter, Granberg makes some suggestions to the church for avoiding future divorces. In what *specific* and *practical* ways could each of the following be accomplished in your home and/or church?

a. "Today's rampant individualism, which glorifies self-assertion and defines self-fulfillment as freedom to indulge one's self whimsically, must be shown by the church to be the perversion it is."

b. "Today's young people need . . . clear teaching on Christian marriage to provide an alternative to the secular world's ideas concerning sex and marriage which they absorb almost by osmosis."

QUESTIONS FOR CHURCH LEADERS

8. Read the last sentence in Granberg's chapter. Are the three goals which he proposes specific enough or are they too vague? How can the goals be made more specific and viable? What would be your first steps in attaining these goals? What would be subsequent steps?

Chapter 8: Andre Bustanoby
Rapid Treatment for a Troubled Marriage

PREPARATION

1. Andre Bustanoby's chapter deals with marriage counseling, but many of the ideas in the chapter could be helpful for couples whose marriages are not troubled. As you read, ask yourself "How can the writer's conclusions be applied to me and my marriage?"

2. The chapter makes a passing reference to 1 Peter 3. Read verses 1–7 and consider how this Scripture could apply to your marriage to keep it from being troubled.

MEETING TOGETHER

3. In his chapter on treatment, Bustanoby makes references to commitment, communication, confrontation, contracts, and centricity. Consider each of these beginning with commitment. It is the author's opinion that for marriages to improve, the couple must be *"committed to making the marriage work and . . . willing to accept responsibility* for making it work." Is a lack of commitment and an unwillingness to accept responsibility at the basis for many marriage tensions? Are you committed to making your marriage work? How are you demonstrating that commitment to your spouse?

4. Communication failures, as we have seen in a previous chapter, is at the basis of many marriage difficulties. What are Bustanoby's "basic rules" for effective communication? Could these work in your marriage? Are they necessary for effective communication?

5. Is it OK for Christian couples to argue? What are the characteristics of a fair fight? According to Bustanoby the best way for a couple to confront each other is for each to say in a nonattacking way what he or she is feeling. The spouse's response is not to get defensive or make excuses. You don't even have to "agree with the facts, but you must agree that the person feels as he says he does." How do you react to this suggestion? Have you tried it in your marriage?

6. The last stage in Bustanoby's treatment program involves making contracts for change. What is the difference between learning contracts and action contracts? Can a couple put these into operation in their own marriage? In what specific ways could this be done in your marriage?

7. Can a nonprofessional counselor use Bustanoby's methods for helping others? How can this be done in the church?

8. How do troubled marriages get treated in your church? Are couples with problems ignored, criticized, or really helped? Are the church leaders interested in helping couples, willing to do so, or capable? How could marriages in your church and community receive better help than they are getting now? Would Bustanoby's method be of practical benefit?

Chapter 9: Donald F. Tweedie, Jr.
A Model for Marital Therapy

PREPARATION

1. In this chapter, Donald Tweedie, who is a professional counselor, takes us right to the heart of the issue of marriage counseling. He begins with an overview of the several approaches that counselors use, followed by his own suggested techniques. As you read, ask yourself, "How could these different approaches help a troubled marriage to improve? How would they work with my marriage?"

2. Tweedie makes a reference to 1 Corinthians 10:24. Read this verse in your Bible, followed by verse 33, then 1 Corinthians 13. In what ways do these passages have a bearing on marriage and marriage counseling?

MEETING TOGETHER

3. Tweedie's chapter gives a concise look at present-day marriage counseling, but at times the author is technical. Does everyone in the group understand what is meant by contract-covenant therapy? If not one or two group members should summarize this approach.

4. Tweedie likens many marriage tensions to labor-management disputes that must be settled by negotiation and arbitration. Do you think contract therapy is really a form of bargaining for an agreement between husband and wife? Is there anything wrong with this way of viewing marriage counseling? If you don't like this perspective can you think of a better, more workable approach to helping troubled marriages?

5. When problems arise in marriage, our feelings often "get hurt" and we yell at one another. Is this an acceptable way to handle disputes? How do you respond to Tweedie's suggestion that it is more realistic to

change behavior rather than trying to change feelings? How would this work in your marriage when disagreements arise? Can you think of examples in your marriage where behavior change was or might have been the best approach to use?

6. Contract therapy promotes "the explicit self-interest" of the husband and wife. The negotiator helps "each spouse get 'the best deal' possible, consonant with personal desires and the common aim." Although Tweedie calls this a "biblical counseling technique developed from a biblical perspective" he openly acknowledges that some Christians disagree. How do *you* react to the criticism that contract therapy "appeals to personal privilege and caters to personal self-interest in a way that is contrary to Christian ethics"? Would contract therapy work in your marriage? Can you and your spouse use it (without a counselor) to help settle disagreements? If not, can you think of a better way to solve problems in the home?

QUESTIONS FOR CHURCH LEADERS

7. Could contract therapy be used to help troubled marriages in your church? What other marriage counseling approaches might be as good or better? Is the Tweedie method better for your church than the approach suggested by Bustanoby in the previous chapter? Why/or why not?

Chapter 10. Norman G. Wakefield
Training Christian Couples for Marriage Counseling

PREPARATION

1. If you had a personal or marriage problem, to whom would you go for help? Think about this before reading farther. . . . The chances are good that you thought of a friend or relative, rather than a professional counselor. Can you think of reasons why a couple in need might prefer to talk to someone they know? Why might they prefer to counsel with a stranger? What potential do you and your spouse have for lay marriage counseling? Discuss this together.

2. Are there biblical grounds for lay counseling? Look up Galatians 6:1, 2 and Romans 12:10–15. Might James 2:14–26 also be relevant?

MEETING TOGETHER

3. The following statements are taken from the first two paragraphs of Norman Wakefield's chapter. Do you agree or disagree? Give reasons for your answers.

a. "Every couple should have friends with whom they can talk over their marital problems and adjustments."

b. "Counselors urgently needed. . . . Not only is there a need for professional counselors, but perhaps an even greater need exists for trained lay counselors who can provide assistance for those who do not have the financial resources for, in-depth need of, or access to a professional counselor."

4. Can you think of advantages and disadvantages to lay counseling?

5. How can an individual or couple determine if they have potential to be lay counselors? What guidelines for selecting lay counselors are given by Wakefield in his chapter? Can you think of others?

6. Do you think there could be some dangers involved in laymen doing counseling? What are these? How could they be avoided?

7. How could Christian couples be (a) trained and (b) used to do counseling in your church and community? Be specific in your answer.

QUESTIONS FOR CHURCH LEADERS

8. Could Christian couples be trained and used for premarital and marriage counseling in your church? If so, how would you train and use them? Would the presence of such couples be threatening to you and your work as a church leader? Try to be honest and specific in answering these questions. Having read Wakefield's chapter, what (if anything) do you plan to do in order to initiate a lay counseling program in your church?

Chapter 11: H. Norman Wright
The Church and Marriage Enrichment

PREPARATION

1. Norman Wright discusses some practical ways by which the church can enrich marriages. Let us begin, however, with *your* marriage. Turn to page 151 and jot down answers to the five evaluation questions. Ask your spouse to do the same, then share and discuss your answers.

2. In his chapter, Wright suggests that a good definition of maturity is found in the book of Galatians. Turn in your Bible to Galatians 5 and read verses 22–26. If these verses described you, how would your marriage and family be affected? How does one get the characteristics that are listed in this passage of scripture?

MEETING TOGETHER

3. At the beginning of his chapter, Wright quotes some disturbing statistics about the high divorce rate. Why are marriages today so unstable? He also quotes Richard Lessor's statement that "today in place of exerting consistent effort and determination to make one's marriage work the solution is to 'bail out.'" Why do people, including Christians, "bail out" instead of working on their marriages?

4. Wright suggests that a church marriage enrichment program should begin by asking the questions, What is our goal? What are we trying to accomplish? Apply these questions to your own marriages. What specific goal or goals do *you* have for *your* marriage? Share these goals with the group. How many persons in the group never have thought previously about goals for their own marriages and families? Is this aimless drifting one of the reasons for boredom and lack of enrichment in marriage?

5. The chapter lists a number of "marriageability traits." What are these? How can they be developed in church members? How can they be developed in you?

6. Turn to Wright's definition of a Christian marriage and ask someone to read it aloud to the group. Are the characteristics described in this definition really essential for Christian marriage? If so, what specific steps can we take to make our marriages more Christian?

7. Based on your reading of Wright's chapter, discuss the ways in which your church could develop a program to enrich marriages within the congregation. Remember that "the problem is not with the institution of marriage itself. The problem centers with individuals . . . and their attitudes." What would be some first steps for bringing about such a program to change individuals and their marriages?

QUESTIONS FOR CHURCH LEADERS

8. In his chapter the author proposes that laymen (in this case couples within the church) should be involved in helping other couples to improve their marriages. What is your opinion of such lay counseling? How would the lay counselors be trained? What is your church doing to enrich marriages? What could and should your church be doing? What is your role in this?

Chapter 12: John Scanzoni
A Christian Perspective on
Alternative Styles of Marriage

PREPARATION

1. What is meant by TFF—the Traditional Family Forms about which John Scanzoni writes? How do you feel about the fact that many people no longer accept TFF? Is this threatening to you? How will you react if your children reject TFF and adapt one of the Alternative Styles of Marriage (ASM) described by Scanzoni?

2. Turn again to read Ephesians 5:21–33 and 1 Peter 3:1–7. Keep these biblical guidelines in mind as you consider the different ASM.

MEETING TOGETHER

3. According to Scanzoni, an increasing number of persons find TFF inadequate for themselves. What do you think are the reasons for this? Do you agree that "dual-career marriage" will emerge to become more and more prevalent in our society? Do you accept Scanzoni's conclusion that "Christians can welcome the emergence because it is a thoroughly biblical alternative"?

4. In your group, consider each of the following ASM: trial marriage, ad hoc arrangements, singleness, single parenthood, childfree marriage, communal living, group marriage, mate swapping, gay marriage, and dual-career marriage. What are the positive and negative features of each. In which could a committed Christian be involved? Give reasons for your answers.

5. In this chapter, Scanzoni raises a very basic question: "What constitutes marriage?" How would you answer this question? Is a ceremony required for marriage? Is sexual intercourse a prerequisite? Is a legally unmarried couple who has sexual intercourse married in God's sight (See 1 Cor. 6:16). Can there be such a thing as "private marriage"?

6. According to Scanzoni, "Many Christians believe that coitus prior to marriage is not God's will for Christians. Others might take a more permissive view and allow it under certain conditions—e.g., unmarried couples close to marriage." What is your view of premarital sex? How would you defend your view (biblically and logically) if you were challenged by some person who had a different view?

7. Think back over this entire book. What problems or aspects of

marriage have not been discussed in the preceding pages? What have you learned about marriage in general? What have you learned about your own marriage?

QUESTIONS FOR CHURCH LEADERS

8. Has your church leadership given any consideration to ways in which you could minister to people who reject TFF? What could you do for these people that you are not doing now? How would you counsel with some young person who has decided that ASM are better than TFF? Do you think it would be helpful for the young people in your church to read and discuss this chapter?

9. In what specific and practical ways is your ministry going to change as a result of this book?

From the Continental Congress on the Family
Make More of Your Marriage

Is it possible to be happily married today—or is marriage as we know it on the way out?

The writers in *Make More of Your Marriage* are convinced that marriage—though it may be changing—is here to stay. And they offer many positive and practical suggestions on how to improve it—how to be happy while married. They consider such provocative questions as:

- what causes most marriages to fail?
- what are the biblical standards for marriage?
- what place should traditional male and female roles have in a Christian marriage?
- how can marriage partners help each other discover their gifts and develop their potential?
- what can churches do to help members improve their marriages?

The chapters were originally prepared for the Continental Congress on the Family. They have been edited for this volume by Gary Collins, who has also provided a study guide designed both for group discussion and to help church leaders rethink their ministry to marriage people in the church and the community.

The authors were selected because of their professional expertise, their Christian faith, and their commitment to helping others make the most of their marriages. They and their subjects are:

LLOYD OGILVIE—Marriage As It Was Meant to Be
LOUIS and COLLEEN EVANS—Gifts of the Spirit in Marriage
LARRY CHRISTENSON—A New Look at Christian Husbands
GLADYS M. HUNT—A New Look at Christian Wives
MARK W. LEE—Reasons Marriages Fail—Communication
DWIGHT H. SMALL—Divorce and Remarriage: A Fresh Biblical Perspective
LARS I. GRANBERG—Divorce and Remarriage: Practical Implications for the Church
ANDRE BUSTANOBY—Rapid Treatment for a Troubled Marriage
DONALD F. TWEEDIE, JR.—A Model for Marital Therapy
NORMAN G. WAKEFIELD—Training Christian Couples for Marriage Counseling
H. NORMAN WRIGHT—The Church and Marriage Enrichment
JOHN SCANZONI—A Christian Perspective on Alternative Styles of Marriage

Editor GARY COLLINS was program director of the Congress on the Family. He is professor of psychology at Trinity Evangelical Divinity School, Deerfield, Ill., and the author of several books on psychology and counseling. He and his wife Julie have two daughters.

WORD BOOKS, Publisher
Waco, Texas 76703

98077
ISBN 0-87680-849-6